CONFESSIONS OF A

Video Vixen

CONFESSIONS OF A
Video Vixen

Karrine Steffans

Amistad
An Imprint of HarperCollinsPublishers

This book is dedicated to my son, Naiim.
Thank you for coming here
and saving my life.

A hardcover edition of this book was published in 2005 by Amistad,
an imprint of HarperCollins Publishers.

HarperCollins books may be purchased for educational, business, or
sales promotional use. For information, please e-mail the Special
Markets Department at SPsales@harpercollins.com.

First Amistad paperback edition published 2006.

Designed by Betty Lew

The Library of Congress has cataloged the hardcover edition as follows:

Steffans, Karrine, 1978–
     Confessions of a video vixen / Karrine Steffans.—1st ed.
       p. cm.
     ISBN-13: 978-0-06-084242-0
     ISBN-10: 0-06-084242-3
       1. Steffans, Karrine, 1978– . 2. Actors—United States—
Biography. 3. Stripteasers—United States—Biography. I. Title.
PN2287.S6765 A3 2005   2005048176
791.4302/8/092B 22

ISBN-13: 978-0-06-089248-7 (pbk.)
ISBN-10: 0-06-089248-X

19 20 21 ❖/LSC 20 19 18 17

Acknowledgments

Confessions are tricky. Many times, as you're confessing something to another person, you discover some new, valuable lesson about yourself. The journey to making this book possible has been a lifelong one. I have been blessed with people who believed in me—one or two have been with me from the very beginning, others have joined me only recently.

I have to thank, before all, God. The blessings that He has allowed me are unbelievable. I am grateful for His presence in my life and in the life of my son. Without God, I never could have made it this far. And for that, I am overwhelmingly grateful.

My son. I credit him with saving my life and with keeping me humble. He is my biggest blessing, and I am completed by him. There aren't enough words to thank him. I am nothing without him. One day, he'll read this, and all I want my son to know is that everything I have done, ultimately, I have done for him. We made it, Man!

There are no words to express the way I feel about my grandmother. Vivian Ovesen is an amazing woman, and no matter the distance between us, she will forever be part of my life.

St. Thomas, itself, deserves its own accolades. The simplicity of the island taught me about the beauty of less. I have come a long way from that twenty-eight-square-mile island in the Atlantic, but though you can take the girl out of the island, you can never take the island out of the girl. Thank God for that.

Thank you to my spiritual adviser and spiritual mother, Deneen Davis. You have been there every step of the way. I know God placed you in my life to help me be a better woman and mother. I will love and appreciate you all of my life.

Damon Dash, Andre Harrell, and Shakim Compere. You three were the first to let me know that my story mattered. I appreciate you all for that.

To my dearest girlfriends, Alicia, Angie, and Cecily. We've stuck together over the past decade, and I appreciate all of you for your acceptance, patience, and for the contributions that you all have made to my life. Thank you.

To the Soumares, and to Loretta and family. Thank you for helping me raise my son over the years. You were all there for us when we needed you and were instrumental to helping my life come together, by keeping my son safe and happy.

Deena, Lashauna, Damon, Ehrich, George, Gina, Jamal, Jawn, John, Terry, Tim, and anyone I may have forgotten. Thanks for being there when I needed you.

To my Papa. Thank you for all the years that you have stood by me, never judging, never turning your back on me. You were the voice in my head, telling me to change and reminding me of all the reasons why. You, above all, are my friend.

To Ice-T. Thank you for changing my life. You gave me the option of leaving my past behind. You gave me a place to go. You opened the doors of Los Angeles to me. I remember everything that you've ever told me. Thank you for being there for me and my son.

I would like to give a special thank-you to all who made *Confessions of a Video Vixen* possible. Gilda Squire, for sharing my vision and for pushing to make this happen. Dawn Davis, for believing in me and in the importance of my life's message. Mark Jackson, for his keen eye and passion. Everyone at Amistad and HarperCollins who contributed to the process and completion of *Confessions*. Also, thank you Karen Hunter for your assistance and expertise.

CONTENTS

x

Introduction

No Shame in My Game

Like so many young girls, I grew up wanting to be famous. I used to watch television and dream about the Beverly Hills lifestyle seen in all of my favorite films. I wanted to live below that HOLLYWOOD sign and drive down Sunset Boulevard and over Mullholland Drive in a Mercedes-Benz while wearing a designer scarf and huge black sunglasses. I wanted to be known by the rich and famous and be seen lunching with the *in* crowd. I wanted to live where they lived and do what they do. I wanted to belong.

I reached most of my goals, but I didn't do it in a conventional way. I did it using the oldest trick in the book. Sex. I am not always proud of what I did, and there are things that I would do over if I could. But I made the best out of what I started with—an abusive mother and an absent father. I didn't write this book to excuse my past. I sat down to write this book because I think my story can serve as a warning to anyone aspiring to the kind of life I have led, and there are plenty of young people trying to do just that. Where young girls once aspired to be models and ballerinas, they now aspire to be hip hop video girls, the next hot girl in the hottest artist's video. Having lived that life, I can say it's not everything it's cracked up to be.

My hips have swayed and popped on MTV while I danced on tabletops and poolside in some of your favorite videos. I've had sex with some of the most delicious and insatiable men in the world. Heads of music labels, NBA stars, and Hollywood's A-list—to say nothing of the emperors of hip hop. But there's an underside—if sex and drugs went hand in hand with rock and roll, they are just as rampant in hip hop. I wouldn't call this book a tell-*all* since there are many details I have kept to myself for the sake of not embarrassing some of the people still associated with me. Details such as which one of my music industry suitors I caught in bed with his male lover and which one of my NBA exes often kept track of me by using the OnStar device placed in the Mercedes-Benz he bought me, many times sending his associates to retrieve me from vacations and nights on the town.

Yet, in the middle of this wild ride that I call my life, I was met with challenges which could have ruined me, if it had not been for the power of change. I am writing my story because I have seen too many fourteen-year-old girls dressed up like their favorite pop icons and young women dying to be thin or saving up for the new pair of breast implants that they are sure will make them stars. Young women who look up to me and women like me and ask to be plugged into the same circles I desperately tried to escape. I have so much firsthand information to offer, and need those young women to know that there are other directions to take. There are always better choices than most of the ones being offered to women today, better choices than the ones I have made.

The top reason a woman finds herself in a rap video, sprawled undressed over a luxury car while a rapper is saying lewd things about her, is a lack of self-esteem. I know it sounds like a cliché, but no one who values, loves, or knows herself would allow herself to be placed in such a degrading position. Finding myself and learning to value who I am was one of the biggest hurdles I had to overcome.

Before my "video girl" career, I was known in some circles as a stripper. Others knew me as "Superhead," the insatiable lover of many Hollywood stars, sports figures, and some of music's most influential performers and executives. None of that is who I really am, nor does it tell the whole story.

Along my journey, there are things that I have seen and overheard which could tarnish and even demolish the reputations of some of these artists. I realized then that I had a power which had nothing to do with my body or my looks or my sexuality. I had information usually confined to members of the "Good Ol' Boys" clubs of the industry. I had been allowed behind those doors, as a modern-day Mata Hari.

The days of MC Lyte, Yo-Yo, Sister Souljah, and Salt-n-Pepa have faded away. Our Queen, Latifah, has broken new ground in another sector, but has left her place on the throne of hip hop empty, waiting to be filled. We live in a world where the only goals at the end of the day are profit and top-ten spots on the *Billboard* charts. Members of the industry are being rewarded for selling the most records, destroying in the process the most beautiful thing about us as a culture—our girls and young women. It was so easy to be drawn in and dominated by it all.

Music videos occupied only a short year and a half of my life, but the picture and the purpose are much larger than that. Magazines, music videos, films, and television continuously fill the heads of young girls with visions of perfect bodies, sex, and money. Parents are often either absent or uneducated or both, rendering them largely unaware of what's going on right in their own living rooms. That little girl whose head was filled with those deceptive visions of wealth and fame is me, all grown up and ready to tell what I know.

Chapter One

DEATH AND LIFE

OCTOBER 2001. I was lying on the hard, cold floor in the bathroom of the famous Chinese bistro Mr. Chow in Beverly Hills. It is one of the most upscale and renowned restaurants in the world, yet I was at the lowest point of my life. With my head next to the toilet, I was alone, in debt, with no friends and no hope.

It had been a long, hard trip that led to this fall. It was a wild roller-coaster ride which included some of the hottest names in hip hop and Hollywood. For two years I rode it out. I was in the middle of it all—dining with P. Diddy, partying with Vin Diesel, going one-on-one with Shaquille O'Neal.

I had money, three cars, a condo in a prestigious neighborhood, a nanny for my son. I had starred in some of the hottest music videos with Jay-Z, LL Cool J, Ja Rule, and Ludacris. I had even costarred in the blockbuster film *A Man Apart*, opposite Vin Diesel. But here I lay on a cold bathroom floor, hugging the toilet's frigid porcelain, completely hopeless. I was broke, homeless, and probably dying.

The last thing I remembered was my body shaking violently as I sat on the toilet with my head in my hands and my friend Eva hovering over me asking me if I was okay. But now I was on the floor and she was gone. *Can I move?* was the only thought swirling through my head.

I tried to say something to make sure I was alive. I couldn't. I tried to move my leg, and it worked. I stood up gingerly and made my way to the sink. I looked around the small, one-stall bathroom. It was dimly lit and tiny, yet elegant. I held on to the sink, looking at myself in the mirror. My pupils were fully dilated, and I could feel my knees wobbling beneath me. I splashed cold water on my face, hoping to snap out of the trouble I was so obviously in.

I looked at my jewelry and clothes. I still wore the diamond-heart pendant and the canary yellow diamond earrings that my ex-husband had given me years before. My ring and bracelet were gifts purchased at Tiffany. My long nails were perfectly French-manicured, and my hair was long and black. My skin had been tanned by the Miami sun and my eyes were gray thanks to my colored contacts. My face was made up to perfection, compliments of MAC and Chanel. My jeans were a two-hundred-dollar pair by fashion icon Marc Jacobs, and the rest of the ensemble followed suit. Everything was designer-made, from my jewelry to my makeup to the clothes I wore—even the drugs I'd consumed.

The next thing I knew, I was on the floor again. When I came to from another bout of convulsions, my tongue was swollen and bloody. I crawled up from the floor and made my way back to the sink to splash more water on my face. I desperately wanted someone to walk in and help, but no one came. I began to panic, with thoughts of the late actor River Phoenix racing through my head. Thoughts of him seizing outside of the Viper Room not too far from where I was, on Sunset Boulevard, right before dying.

I thought of how awful it would be if I died in the bathroom at Mr. Chow. I thought of the irony of it all—of the paparazzi waiting outside for Nicolas Cage and LL Cool J, who were both in the dining area eating with friends. I thought of how pretty and rich I looked, yet my life had become ugly and poor. But the most prominent thought was of my son, Naiim. My nanny hadn't heard from me in months and had no idea how to find me. No one even knew my real name or where I lived or who my family was or where I came from. To them, my name was Yizette, a name that I had made up when I was sixteen, during my years as a stripper.

I thought of Naiim and wanted to live. I thought if I screamed his name as loud as I could, God would hear me and allow me another chance at being a mother. God had to know that despite everything I had done until this point, I loved my son and I wanted to do right by him.

I stumbled to the bathroom door, opened it, and began to scream his name into the stairwell that led downstairs into the main dining area of the restaurant. I screamed his name over and over until my voice was gone. No one heard me. I stumbled back into the restroom to splash more water on my face, hoping the water alone would be enough to reverse what I had done. My heart was racing, and its beat was all I could hear in my head. There were sweat beads on my face. My mouth was dry and my vision blurred. My body went into convulsions three, four more times, each time landing me on the cold hard tile. No one was there for me. I was going to die alone.

One year earlier, no one could have told me that my life would turn out that way. I was invited to a function one Friday night in October 2000 at the Sky Bar, located on Sunset Strip. I reluctantly met an acquaintance there and quickly began to mingle, in order to make the best out of what promised to be a boring evening. The crowd was very stuffy, and I found myself yawning in between conversations with a concert pianist and a score composer. After about an hour of walking around, sampling the vast array of mediocre hors d'oeuvres and oversize apple martinis, I was ready to go. As I searched for the acquaintance who'd brought me to the event, he came up behind me, grabbed my arm, and pulled me toward the pool.

"I want you to meet someone," he said. "Gary, this is Yizette. Yizette, this is Gary."

As I said before, Yizette was a name and persona I made up when I was sixteen, after I ran away from my father and wanted a new identity and, hopefully, a new life. I landed in Los Angeles.

Gary was handsome, dressed all in black, and of medium

build and height. He was soft-spoken and reserved. As we began to talk, we realized that we shared the same sentiments about the function we were attending. We laughed at each other's silly anecdotes and soon found ourselves exchanging phone numbers. After the function, we all headed over to a local club called Nora's Café. There we continued to sip martinis, and at one point I am sure I climbed on top of a table and started dancing. It was a night to remember. But by the following morning, I had forgotten most of it.

The next afternoon, when I had finally recovered from the night before, I checked my messages to find one from Gary. Initially, I couldn't remember who Gary was among the sea of people I had met at the Sky Bar and at Nora's Café. After a brief moment of recollection, I began to connect the voice with the face. I failed, however, to return the call. That Sunday, while I was driving around in West Los Angeles, my cell phone rang. The number was unfamiliar to me, so I answered with caution.

"Hey, Yizette. . . . This is Gary, from the other night," the voice said.

I rolled my eyes in silent response. I was used to men hitting on me and thought that Gary was just another example. But I was wrong. What Gary said next would not only surprise me, it would change my life.

He began to explain to me that he was a film director, and he was in the beginning stages of production on his new film. He wanted me to pick up a copy of the script and read for him. He said there was a part he thought would be perfect for me. I was unsure what to think and actually doubted that he was a director of any substance. After you've lived in Los Angeles for a while, you begin to take what people say they do with a grain of salt, particularly in Hollywood. Still, that Monday, I went to the address he gave me on Beverly Boulevard. I arrived at the production office and picked up the script. Once in my car, I began to read it and was baffled because the character I was to be reading for, Candice Hicks, appeared nowhere in the script.

The very next day I was called to read on-camera for Gary and the producers. I read lines for another character while trying to conceal my nervous stomach and dry mouth. Just as with many other things, I performed without thought. I read the lines through a few times and that was it. I was done.

Gary walked me out to the hallway and thanked me for coming by. I was still unsure of what I had just done, what it was really for, and who I was dealing with. But I began to get a clue once he mentioned that I was up for the role of the wife of Larenz Tate's character. Larenz Tate was a name I knew from his previous movies, so the project became a bit more legitimate and real. Had I known how big this opportunity really was, I might not have gotten through the audition.

On the Thursday after we met, I received a call from Gary's production office telling me I had been cast as Candice Hicks, the wife of Demetrius Hicks, played by Larenz Tate. They said the part would have to be written for me. I was thrilled. Although I had acted all throughout my school years, and being in films was something I had always dreamed of, it was never something that I felt was an achievable goal. But here it was.

After I'd digested everything Gary's crew told me, it finally hit me—Gary was famed director F. Gary Gray—who had done *Set It Off, Friday,* and *The Negotiator,* and would go on to direct *The Italian Job* and *Be Cool.* I was going to be part of a big-budget New Line Cinema production. When I left my sad life and ran to Los Angeles, I had no idea what I would be doing. I had no idea how I was going to survive. For me, being part of a film was much more than surviving, it was a move toward succeeding.

On the following Monday, just a week and a half after meeting Gary, I showed up for my first table reading with the entire cast. Gary sat at the head of the table, and Larenz sat directly across from me. I didn't recognize many of the actors there but was secretly drawn to a tall, muscular man sitting directly to my right. His voice was overwhelmingly powerful, yet his demeanor was gentle. From time to time, his shoulder brushed against mine, and I would get a rush. My attraction to this man was strong. His name was Vin Diesel.

Coincidentally, my first film shoot would take place just a few blocks away from the house where I'd shot my first music video. We began shooting *A Man Apart* at Zuma Beach in Malibu. I awakened at three in the morning and got in my car to drive to the set. I glided into Malibu by way of the well-known, picturesque calm of the Pacific Coast Highway, with the windows in my car down so I could feel the air, brisk and moist with dew. I was blasting my radio and sang along, loudly, with every song during the one-hour drive from my condo. I arrived on the set and headed directly to the catering truck for a breakfast burrito then sat in the hair and makeup trailer. I was officially an actress. I felt that everything I had done up until that point, everything that had happened to me—from my abusive childhood, the rape, being a teen runaway, the stripping—had not stopped me or beaten me. I had reinvented myself. I was moving on and, hopefully, moving up.

Perhaps when one has a difficult start in life, the universe has a way of balancing everything out. I do believe that every cloud has a rainbow and a silver lining. I have had many, many clouds—more than most.

Chapter Two

THE SINS OF THE MOTHER

I HATE MY MOTHER. Those are strong words that are forbidden and shunned by God, and I struggle with this emotion every day of my life. But it's how I feel. As a child, while I would see other children long for their mothers, cling to their mothers, cry for their mothers, I was glad when my mother was away. I hated to be near mine. I hated to hear her voice and would feel nauseous, anticipating her return home from work.

I cringed when she was in the same room with me and looked forward to bedtime because that meant, at least for the day, my time with her was over. I was fully aware of these feelings as early as three years old. It seems almost unnatural for a child to despise the woman who gave him or her life. But my life was different, and I knew I wasn't like other children.

My mother is beautiful. She is a one-woman melting pot of Puerto Rican, Jamaican, and Danish heritage. I remember her skin as being slightly tanned and her hair thick and wavy. She walked with a switch and a sway, and everywhere she went, men followed. She bathed herself in perfume and wore tight-fitting clothes. She adorned herself with twenty-four-karat gold. She was never without a man—somebody's man. But even with all of her beauty and charm, there was another side to Josephine.

She was a very unhappy woman who didn't have any female friends. She based her whole existence on the ability to get a man, and she always seemed unhappy because one of these men who she so desperately needed in her life had "done her wrong." There was a revolving door of men when I was growing up. Some of them even came back for seconds and thirds, but none of them ever stayed. I knew she loved my father and wanted to be with him, but he, too, didn't stay. His time with her seemed to be just that . . . time. And time makes things change.

I witnessed my mother running around town, aimlessly. I would hear the women around town talk about her. It usually followed a complimentary comment about me. "Karrine, she's so smart. You know, she's the only one to score a hundred on her test last week! But that mother of hers . . . I heard she was seen with so-and-so's husband."

Eventually, my two sisters came along, born only a year and a half apart. We were all bastards, each of us the product of a different man—men who would never stay, men who would never come back. Men who I was forced to call "uncle," something for which I resented my mother. I never really knew the two men who fathered my sisters. To tell the truth, I don't believe my mother knew them very well, either. She seemed to be in this vicious cycle of trying to keep men in her life by having their babies. After the third child, perhaps she began to get the hint.

I remember vividly, one night I woke up and was startled to realize that I had been removed from the bed and crammed into the crib with my infant sister. My mother was five months pregnant with my youngest sister. I immediately figured that my mother needed the bed.

There was a backdoor in our room that led to the backyard. It was perfect for my mother, who had been sneaking men in and out of this door nearly her entire life. I couldn't make out what was being said, but the tone of the whispers was heavy. Just as my vision had thoroughly adjusted, I realized the man standing in the doorway must have been the father of the baby she was carrying. I blinked a few times, wanting to get a better look, and tried to make out what was being said.

My mother was begging, "No, don't go! Don't go!"

Her hands were wrapped around his wrists and the two of them were caught in a sort of tug-of-war. My mother lost the battle, as he wriggled free and charged out the door. It looked like a scene out of *Gone With the Wind* as my mother's rounded silhouette crouched to the floor in agony, crying. I was almost eight years old and I can remember not feeling at all sorry for her. In fact, I was a little happy. She deserved to feel the same sort of pain she had inflicted upon those around her, including me.

I was so embarrassed to be my mother's daughter.

When I heard the women talk about her at my school and in the streets, I hung my head in shame. And as much as I hated my mother, I believe she felt the same way about me.

I was a reminder to her of everything she could not be—I was young and had my whole life ahead of me. I was smart and the entire island where I grew up acknowledged me. I was my father's daughter, and around the island, even though he had long since left, people remembered him. He had owned a few businesses on the island and employed many people. My father was charismatic, and because he was from New York, he'd stood out on the tiny island. I would hear stories about how handsome and smart and witty he was. A woman once stopped us in the street and said I was beautiful and that I looked just like him. As she walked away, my mother pulled me to the side and said, "She's lying. She's just saying that because she used to like your father."

My mother always made me feel I was less than a person. She despised the fact that I received constant praise and she was worthy of none. Before I was born, she was the center and now I had taken her shine. We were in competition from the day I arrived. My purpose in life was supposed to be to keep my father with her, to make him love her. But a one-night stand is just that, no matter how long it lasts. The mistake he made wasn't leaving her, but leaving me with her.

I was born in 1978 on a hot, sticky late-August day on the twenty-eight-square-mile island of St. Thomas. My mother was an eighteen-year-old native. My father was twenty-six and lived on the island from 1976 to 1984. After my father went back to his life on Long Island, New York, my mother and I lived with my grandmother Vivian in her four-bedroom house. Along with me, my mother, and grandmother were also my aunt, two cousins, and two uncles. Later came my two younger sisters. In all, there were ten of us sharing four bedrooms. The house had one bathroom, uncovered windows, no hot water, no washing machines, and no air-conditioning.

On most days, we had to boil water for our baths. On those days, my two cousins and I shared the same bathwater. The rule was the youngest bathed first, which was one of the few times being the youngest paid off for me. But sometimes there was no time to boil water and that's when we took cold showers, and took them very quickly.

My grandmother would wash all of the clothes by hand. Everything. Towels and sheets, jeans and shirts. Everyone was supposed to wash their own clothes, but my grandmother could often be seen outside with two large barrels washing everyone's clothes. Then they would be hung out to dry on the wire lines she had tied between two poles in the backyard. The bathroom was small and run-down, as was most of the house. The water supply was prepaid and delivered to the house by a water truck, which funneled the water into the cistern below the house. Because of this, we weren't allowed to use much water, so we kept empty buckets outside to save rainwater and even saved bathwater in order to flush the toilet. My grandmother saw no sense in flushing the clean water that could be used for drinking.

Come winter, spring, or fall, sunshine or hurricane, the windows to our house always seemed to be open. They were actually louvers, metal shutters with a turning handle which would open them. There was no glass or screens to protect the house from insects or even large animals. It was not unusual to come home to a bat or a tarantula, a stray cat, dog, or chicken in the house. It was common to just chase them into the backyard.

The backyard was like another world, filled with fruit trees like banana, papaya, guava, avocado, and passion fruit. Stray animals lived back there surrounded by a plethora of herbs that my grandmother would boil down to make home remedies for any and all ailments. This was the way life was there. It was normal. It was also normal for my grandmother to take care of us all. My mother would stay out all night, sometimes not returning for days at a time. But my grandmother Vivian was always there. I called her "Ma." She encouraged me and she supported me.

I was a smart kid, well known for my academic achievements. I was always featured in the school plays and showcases. When the Stouffers Corporation built a resort on the island's waterfront in 1983, I was invited to recite poems I had written and to cut the ribbon at the opening ceremony. My grandmother was there. My mother was not. My mother never came to any of my events. It was my grandmother who made sure that every time I performed, I had shiny, new patent-leather shoes and a brand-new dress. She was adamant that no one ever saw me in the same dress twice. My grandmother was strict, but it was evident that she loved me.

The relationship between my grandmother and my mother was quite a different story. There was something there and I was never sure what it was. My grandmother Vivian had seven children, some from different fathers. My mother was the youngest and the sibling with the fairest complexion, something that was obviously an issue among the sisters. I believe that my mother's father, Axel, was the only man who had married my grandmother, and my mother played that card as often as possible. In her mind, being light-skinned and the only nonbastard of the seven made her superior to the others. If my grandmother did show any favor at all, it may have been only because my mother was the baby, the last born of her seven children. It is my belief that it was the favor my mother was shown outside of the house which made her feel superior, and in turn, my aunts resented her. By the time I was born, the damage between my aunts and my mother had been done. Even as a young child, I could feel the tension. To this day, none of my aunts speaks to my mother and neither does my grandmother.

As I got older, it seemed like my relationship with my mother grew more and more contentious. She became more impatient and more brutal toward me. One day after school, right after my first sister was born, I went to meet my mother at her job at a little clothing store called Marrianne's. As I was leaving to walk home, I noticed a woman in a car parked outside next to the sidewalk. She called me over and asked if my mother had a baby boy or a girl. Being seven, I answered the question truthfully—"A girl"—and continued on my way home. Not even thirty minutes after

I got into the house, my mother came barreling through the door. A sinking feeling came over me. Automatically, I knew I was in trouble. I wasn't sure what I had done. But I knew for sure that I was in trouble.

"You are not to tell my business out in the street!" my mother yelled at me. "I don't care who asks you what. You keep your mouth shut!"

No one was at home, and I prayed silently that my grandmother would make it through the door before the first blow of the belt. My mother walked away and came back with a *Webster's World Edition Dictionary*. It was the biggest book I had ever seen as a child. It contained every single word in the English language and many from other parts of the world, including slang. This book must have weighed more than ten pounds. And as she picked it up, I just knew she was going to swing it across my head. I closed my eyes and kept praying for my grandmother to make it home from work.

As I prayed, my mother was still going on about what I had done wrong. It was all too grown-up for me to really understand. I didn't know the rules of engagement between adults. At seven years old, I had no idea what "business" was and why other women were "in" hers! And for this, I was about to get pummeled by *Webster's*.

I felt this heavy weight on top of my head, and opened my eyes to see that my mother had placed the dictionary on my head.

"Get on your knees and balance this until I come back!" she barked. "And you better not move or take this book from your head!"

And then she was gone. I figured she'd left to undo any damage I had done by "telling her business," so I knelt there, still praying. My young rational mind told me to get up from that spot and relax my aching back and knees, and if she did make it back, I had enough time to put the dictionary back on my head and get back into position before she hit the door. It was a brilliant plan and could have most certainly worked, but my frightened, true self had serious doubts. *What if I don't make it back into position in time?* I asked myself. *She'll tear me to shreds and no one will be here to save me.*

This was the least violent punishment I had ever received and I was not going to mess it up. This was a good thing, I told myself. I stayed there, on my knees, with that book on my head, crying and praying for two hours. I was weak and my neck, back, and knees felt like they were breaking with each passing minute. And just as I ran out of tears, my grandmother came through the front door to see me there in the kitchen, struggling to maintain my punishment.

"What the hell?!" she screamed in anguish.

I immediately began to ramble off the events which had led to this scene. As I relived the moments, the tears began to stream again. The look in my grandmother's eyes was so painful. She didn't understand the story and how I could be punished for answering a question honestly—for, essentially, being a child. The hurt in her eyes made me hurt more, and I began to cry less for myself and more for her. It wouldn't be the last time she'd be there to rescue me.

My mother had been a seamstress. I loved making

clothes for my dolls out of her leftover scraps of material. One day, though, I had a better idea. In my drawer was a sock without a mate, white with a lacy ruffle around the edge. My creative brain went to work as I cut the toe from the sock and made a pair of shoulder straps, creating a frilly ball gown for my doll. Somewhere, in the middle of all the excitement, I lost my mother's shears. I hadn't noticed until she came home from work and started looking for them.

She finally asked me, "Have you seen my scissors?! They're not in my sewing box where I left them!"

By the look of sheer terror in my eyes, she could tell that I had done something wrong. So I confessed to making the sock dress. She looked high and I looked low. The scissors were lost, and I couldn't breathe or swallow because my next move could be the end. Just as I had given up on ever finding the orange-handled scissors, I spotted them behind the bed. Why hadn't I seen them there before?

Just as I began to feel relieved that the scissors had been found, I was attacked from behind with a six-inch-wide leather belt. My mother beat me and beat me until my body was on fire. Every lash felt like a thousand. As she beat me, she spewed obscenities and told me how stupid I was. The lashes got more and more severe until the welts opened up and began to ooze blood.

She had stripped me naked and beaten me until my body lay swollen and bloody. I was fading in and out of consciousness. The next thing I remember is my grandmother bursting through the bedroom door, grabbing me by the wrist, throwing me into the shower, and running cold water over my blistering skin. On any other day, I dreaded a cold shower. But on that day, I reveled in it. It felt as if that cold water brought me back to life. As I stood there in the tub catching my breath, I could hear my grandmother and my mother fighting.

My grandmother Vivian was my guardian angel. My mother, to me, was the devil. And while the battle of good against evil played out in the next room, I was in my own personal purgatory in the bathroom. Soon enough, my purgatory would turn into a living hell.

The four of us being crammed into that one room must have taken a toll on my mother. It also seemed that my mother had finally had enough of living on a small island where everyone knew her business. When I was ten years old, we packed up and moved to Florida. We arrived during one of the state's coldest winters, which seemed fitting. I didn't appreciate the change in venue because it took me away from the one person who was always in my corner— my grandmother.

I was in the fifth grade and became a social outcast. I wasn't as pretty as the other girls in my school, I had an accent from my years on the island, and I wasn't the academic standout I'd been back in St. Thomas. This was a much bigger playing field. I was lost, and my mother didn't help.

I remember my fifth-grade banquet. It was the end the school year, and I had gone through the entire semester looking and feeling like a misfit. My clothes were never up-to-date, and I wore the same things over and over. There was hope for me to redeem myself at the banquet because my mother would be making my dress. When she arrived home with a few yards of a peach satin material, I was pleased. I could see myself in a beautiful, feminine peach gown that everyone would adore and envy. As my mother went to work on my dress, I waited and watched. I knew I couldn't tell anyone that my mother was *making* my dress, so when I was asked about it I said that she had bought me a beautiful peach dress from the mall and that it was very expensive.

Three days after my mother had started the dress, it was finished. I raced home to see the finished product. There it was, hanging on the closet door in my room. It was peach, it was frilly, and it was horrible. It looked like a big satin box with sleeves and ruffles. I was mortified. Holding back the tears of disappointment, I tried the dress on as she had instructed, and it fell over my tiny frame like a brown paper bag.

I arrived at the school yard for the banquet with this peach drape hanging from my bony shoulders. I heard the laughter, but I pretended that I didn't. I felt small as I looked around the room at everyone else's dress. I wished I were invisible. As the day went on, I grew increasingly self-conscious and watched the clock, constantly waiting for the banquet to end. Finally, when my mother picked me up that afternoon, she spoke the words which would stay with me forever.

Upon seeing all the other girls' dresses, she said, "See, that's why I made you a dress. I don't want anybody looking at you."

Now that we were far away from the island where I had family and friends who loved and supported me, she could make me look and feel so small no one would notice me. And she did.

However, by the end of my fifth-grade year, someone did notice me. His name was Kevin. I don't remember much about him except he had blond hair and blue eyes, and I thought he was the cutest boy in my class. After school I invited him and another boy, as well as one of my best friends, back with me to my house. There were only about two hours between the time when I got home from school and the time when my mother returned home from work, but I began to find ways to maximize that little block of time. On one afternoon, Kevin gave me my first real kiss. I was ten and a lot of things inside of me would be different from that point on. I would crave the feeling I had the day when he kissed me.

I felt loved. I felt pretty. I was acknowledged, and I wanted more.

Chapter Three

FLOWER OFF THE BLOOM

MY MOTHER HAD BEEN DILIGENT in making sure that my life was as miserable as possible. I was never allowed to leave the apartment for anything other than school. There were no trips to the mall or skating rinks for me—nothing that would help me fit in with the other kids. Still, I eventually started to make friends in my new home of Tampa, to do some activities and have some fun outside the confines of our small two-bedroom apartment.

When I turned thirteen, I found a best friend, Charlene. She was wonderful, and my mother, to my surprise, liked her. She was able to talk my mother into letting me go with her to the mall. Charlene told her that her mother would be picking us up afterward. I couldn't believe that I would be pulling up and walking around without an adult. This was a new, liberating feeling and I liked it. I finally felt normal.

We spent three glorious hours window-shopping, talking, and walking around the mall. Charlene's mother was scheduled to meet us out front in less than three hours. We waited for a while, and then finally, a car slowed to a stop in front of us. I stepped toward the end of the sidewalk, grabbed the door handle, then stopped. It was not Charlene's mother, but a car full of boys I had never met. When I turned to look at Charlene, she was smiling. She greeted each one of the boys by name. They were apparently her friends.

Charlene introduced me to them as she got in the backseat of the car, pulling me along beside her. There were three boys, obviously older than we were, and totally out of my league. That's when it hit me. The story about her mother picking us had been a lie. She had planned this all along without mentioning a word to me. So without any protest, I slammed the car door behind me and we drove off. I trusted my best friend.

Charlene was one of the more popular girls in school. She dressed in the latest fashions and had a confident air about her. I looked up to her and wanted so much to be like her. Her mother would let her do almost anything she wanted and she always told me stories about the places she went and the people she hung out with. Jealous of her life, I did everything I could to be around and fit in with her. Charlene also wore a lot of makeup. I was mesmerized because I wasn't allowed to even wear clear lip gloss. And she knew all about the hottest music. Charlene even gave me my first nickname and we called ourselves sisters. That's what she was to me.

We drove with these boys for what seemed just a short time, but I was unclear about where we were. I hadn't spent a whole lot of time out and about, and even though I lived in this city, I didn't know my way around. We ended up at the apartment of another guy, and in addition to the three who were with us, there were two more guys in the apartment.

After hanging out for a bit, I began to like one of the guys. His name was Roni, and I knew he liked me, too. Everyone in this room was seventeen and older, except for me and Charlene. The boys made me feel comfortable and accepted. So when Roni asked me to follow him, I did, right into the bathroom. It was tiny and cold. He asked me if I had ever had sex before, and I hesitantly answered no. I wasn't sure if this made me cool or not. I was hoping it wouldn't deter him from doing what I thought both he and I wanted to do. To my surprise, I was ready and definitely curious. I stared into his deep green eyes and ran my fingers through his curly black hair. He spoke to me in Spanish as he hoisted my naked body onto the bathroom sink. I was shivering with fright, but also with anticipation.

I felt a rush of adrenaline come over my entire body and I began to sweat. I had never been touched this way before. I couldn't understand how or why I felt so prepared to lose my virginity to this person I had only just met hours before, in a strange bathroom, in a strange apartment, but I was. Somehow it felt empowering. I was drunk with the power of freedom. I wanted to stay out all night and didn't want this feeling to end. It did, though, when the piercing pain of penetration made me realize what I was doing.

Roni placed me on the floor in an attempt to gain better entry, but to no avail. The pain was excruciating, and the pressure from his body crushed me as I became pinned between him and the floor. This was not the romantic scenario I had always envisioned. This was not right. Obviously, Roni had the same feeling because after about fifteen minutes of trying, he gave up. I was relieved, to say the least.

We returned to the living room, where everyone had been drinking and talking during our little experiment in the bathroom. Charlene instantly sat down beside me to get the details. After I told her that nothing really happened, she seemed pleased. What I couldn't have known then was that she had a serious secret crush on Roni and was angered that he liked me. In her mind, I had somehow crossed the line.

There was another guy in the apartment. Everyone called him Rodney. All I can remember about him was that he had extremely dark skin, was not very attractive, and had soulless eyes. After I came out of the bathroom with Roni, I could see in Rodney's eyes that it was now open season on me. Rodney stared at me intensely for a while and I became nervous. I turned to Charlene to ask her if we could leave, and just then, Rodney called Roni into one of the back rooms. I was uncomfortable. I knew that something was terribly wrong.

A few minutes passed, and my legs began to shake. It was getting late and we were supposed to be home by now. If I didn't get home soon, there would be big trouble at my house, and as I expressed this to Charlene, she just blew me off. She didn't understand what kind of trouble went on at my house; she didn't have those kinds of worries and fears. I couldn't go into details about the sort of consequences I would face. It was too embarrassing, so I pretended not to be worried. I managed to keep my legs from shaking and began to drink alcohol along with the rest of the crew.

When Roni and Rodney emerged from the room, the look on their faces was unmistakable. Rodney had given the order, and from that moment on, Roni didn't say another word to me or even look in my direction. Rodney sat down next to me on the sofa and my knees began to knock. For the first time ever, I just wanted to be at home with my mother.

Even though the sight of him was making me sick, he said the words I wanted to hear. "We're going to take you girls home."

It wasn't long before we all piled into the car. It was late; the sun had gone down. I knew I would be in big trouble when I got home, so I began bracing myself for the worst. Whatever the punishment would be, it would be better than being out with these people. As we drove toward my street, I began to feel a bit relieved. Finally, I could see the two-story structure I lived in becoming larger and larger still. Yet as we got closer, the car moved faster. And we sped right past my apartment. I alerted the driver that he had missed a stop.

"My apartment was back there!" I yelled.

Everyone in the car was silent. I was sandwiched between two guys—one of them Rodney—in the backseat.

Charlene was pinned against the back right door, and when I looked over at her, she stared out of the window as if everything was going as planned. I stared out of the window, with my eyes welling with tears.

Then Rodney ordered, "Let's go to the house."

I felt a sense of relief. I could just get out of the car, I could get away. I could run to a public place and get help. I was growing increasingly terrified. I was particularly scared of Rodney. He had that look in his eye. He was harsh and abrasive and the other guys seemed afraid of him. He was in charge and no one in that car would dare stand up to him. I was in trouble and apparently had no allies—not even my best friend.

Eventually, we pulled up to a house. Rodney grabbed my wrist with all his strength and pulled me out of the car. The house was a monstrosity. It was a puzzle of brown boards in a sort of hexagonal shape and its frame stood on top of fifteen-foot stilts. This house had obviously once been someone's dream; now it was abandoned. We had a lot in common, that house and me.

The street we were on was darkened by the lack of working lights. I looked around for a place to run, a house that looked friendly and inviting, a house with no gate to fumble with and no dog to deter me. I was planning my escape.

We ascended the wooden stairway carefully. It seemed as if every other step was missing. The house was rotting with termites, and at the front entrance there was a big gaping hole in the floor, through which the ground fifteen feet below could be seen. As the crew moved past the dangerous obstacles almost without looking, it was clear they had all been there before.

Rodney took me to a corner of the house away from the others. My heart was beating so hard and so loud that I couldn't hear a word he was saying to me. What was clear, though, was the strong hold he still had on my wrist and his slimy tongue wandering around my neck and face. I wanted to throw up on him. He licked and kissed my shivering frame. He lifted my shirt and roughly fondled my underdeveloped breasts before he began to unbutton my jeans. My right hand became numb from the grip he had on me, and I was beginning to cry. I cried silently, and to my disgust, my tears excited him. He began to ravish me, tearing the stitching of my shirt and scratching my skin as he tugged at my pants.

The neighborhood dogs had been barking from the moment we pulled up to the house, and by this time, the neighbors were in their yard. I could hear them talking, wondering what was going on. My silent cries grew louder and eventually turned into a scream.

"Call the police!" I heard from outside. Rodney loosened the grip on my wrist and relocated it to my neck. "Let's go!" was the order and everyone barreled out of the house, down the stairs, and back into the car.

It must have been extremely late because there were no people anywhere as we drove around the city looking for a place to finish the evening. Rodney took hold of my wrist again and now he was mad as hell, with a fire in his eyes.

I could tell by the conversations in the car that Rodney, allegedly only eighteen years old at the time, was a criminal and had spent time in jail. I was terrified and had become almost numb at this point. I stared blankly into space, my breathing slowed, and I went to another place. I was back home on St. Thomas, at my grandmother's house. I was picking the fruit from the trees—bananas, papayas, guavas. I was young again and safe. I could smell my grandmother's fish and rice. I was loved.

The car stopped abruptly when Rodney gave the order. I opened my eyes and saw the motel. I was never going to get out of there, I thought. Rodney got out and unscrewed the bolts of the air-conditioner of a courtyard-style motel room. He pushed the air-conditioning unit into the room, crawled in behind it, and unlocked the door for the rest of us. I just stared into space, a zombie. Exactly what happened after this remains a mystery to me because I was gone, back in a happy place.

I do remember there were two beds in the room—Rodney and I were on one; Charlene, Roni, and the other guy were on another. They were talking and laughing among themselves, as if what was going on in the next bed was not disturbing. I was trapped under the covers by Rodney. As he lay on top of me, his right hand was around my neck, his left hand pulling off my pants.

My next memory is of him inside of me, tearing away at my insides. I screamed and cried simultaneously. I clawed and kicked, tirelessly. He took the hand from my neck and covered my mouth with the same forceful grip he had applied to my wrist. I could feel his hot, moist breath as he panted over me. A puddle of murky sweat pooled under my rib cage and in my navel. He was dirty. His body carried the odor of devious determination. I could feel my virgin skin ripping and the pain sent strobes of light shooting through my head as I overheated from the panic. I couldn't catch my breath and I couldn't fight anymore. He was winning, and I was losing much more than my purity.

My insides weren't as inviting as he would have wanted, so the next memory I have is of him giving Roni the order to hold my legs down while he went to the bathroom. I was shaking and the look in Roni's eyes was pitiful. He knew this was wrong, but he wasn't man enough to face Rodney. A few short seconds later, Rodney returned with something in his hands. He began rubbing his hands together and lather began to form around his rough black fingers. He rubbed soap into my torn flesh in order to gain lubrication. I screamed in agony. It burned as if it were acid being poured directly into my lacerated cavity.

Exhausted and relieved when it was over, I fell asleep. The very next morning, Charlene, who was now no longer afraid to be on my side, and I were the first to awaken. We quietly got dressed and planned our escape. Just then she pointed out to me the hideous hickey Rodney had placed on my neck. That man had thought of any way he could to mark and scar my body, to scar my spirit. Just as we were trying to leave, the others woke up and stopped us from leaving. Rodney didn't try to restrain me from this point on. I guess he had already achieved whatever it was he'd set out to do, and now he was simply hungry. A McDonald's was directly next door, so the plan was for us to walk over for breakfast. Charlene and I looked at each other and knew this would be our only chance to get away. We just needed to run as fast we could. And that's what we did.

As the guys walked toward the counter to order their breakfast, Charlene and I slipped into the bathroom. We took about fifteen seconds to come up with a game plan and immediately put it to work. Opening the door and peeking into the restaurant, we could see that the guys weren't facing in our direction. They were off to the far right of us, in line, and to our near left was the door through which we'd just entered. So as not to bring any attention to ourselves, we calmly walked out of the door to the sidewalk. Then, without saying a word, we both started running as fast as we could.

The guys saw us through the window of the restaurant and began to give chase. By the time they made it out to the sidewalk, we had already hit the first corner. Our hearts stopped when we realized that we had just turned onto a dead-end street. We could hear them running and calling out to us. We had to do something and do it fast. Next to us were a few cars parked along the sidewalk. Again, without saying a word to each other, we instinctively crouched down and slid under one of the cars. Seconds later, the sound of their feet stopped, followed by whispers. I couldn't hear what was being said over the sound of my heart beating, and in an instant they just gave up and walked back toward the McDonald's.

Charlene and I didn't trust the situation, so we waited a few minutes before we moved from under the car, then ran quickly toward the nearest pay phone. Charlene called her mother and told her to pick us up at the corner. When she slammed the phone back onto the receiver, I felt this part of the ordeal was over. But I knew that there would be something just as traumatizing waiting for me at home.

The ride to my house was surprisingly calm. As I sat in the backseat of the car, Charlene and her mother were deep in conversation. What was so surprising was the tone of the discussion. Although her mother was obviously disappointed, she was still kind and loving. She listened. And when it came her turn to speak, she did it with more concern than anger. I wondered if Charlene understood how great she had it, and then I thought about what would happen when I walked through the door at my house. My heart began to race and I was having difficulty breathing.

From the ride in the car to the long walk to the front door, I was blank. I don't remember everything clearly during that short stretch of time, but I do remember my mother answering the door. Without even blinking, she grabbed me by my hair and threw me to the ground. She began to punch and kick my head, neck, and chest.

She screamed, "You smell like sex! You're disgusting! Go take a shower!"

I was waiting for Charlene's mother to jump in and save me, but she and Charlene stood in our front doorway with shocked looks on their faces. Charlene's mother had worked for the child welfare and protection department, so I knew she was accustomed to helping children in my situation. Off duty now, she did nothing as my mother beat blood out of my face right there before her.

My mother never once stopped to ask what had happened. She never once expressed concern or worry about me. Never asked if I was all right. She automatically attacked me and made me feel dirty and low . . . the same way I had felt in that hotel room.

The next thing I remember is being thrown into a scalding shower. There was no punishment that could compare to what I had just endured—being held captive and raped. The near-boiling water hit my skin and I blacked out. I slid down to the floor of the tub and curled into a fetal position. I was so drained and so empty I didn't even cry.

The water washed away the physical evidence of what happened the night before. But the emotional scars would remain. Later that day, I was looking out of my bedroom window, watching the other kids play. Things were back to normal and I was not allowed outside except to go to school. I turned on my radio and there was Patti LaBelle singing "Somebody Loves You." I listened closely to the words of the song. It was the first time I had heard them and it touched me to the core. Oh, how I wanted Patti to be right.

I cried as I watched the kids outside. I wanted to be one of them, happy and free. I wanted to be able to play, to be without worry or fear, but I knew I was different. I was not happy and I would never again be a child.

I did not mature the way I should have. I was always nervous and always afraid. I had no confidence in myself and largely withdrew from everyone. I was so nervous I wet the bed and sucked my thumb constantly up until high school. The bed-wetting happened every night, without fail. Again, my mother was never concerned with the reasons why; she just made me feel bad and disgusting because of it. She verbally attacked me every morning when I woke up in a pool of my own urine, which only made me more nervous. This was a vicious cycle and I wanted out.

Chapter Four

ON THE RUN

WHILE GROWING UP ON THE ISLAND, I was a diligent student and loved school. But almost immediately after we moved to Florida, I became unfocused,
going from a straight-A student to barely being able
to pass my classes. Without the love, support, and
encouragement of my grandmother, I looked for
those things outside of my home. I found what I
thought I had been looking for with the neighborhood kids. We started hanging out during my free
two hours after school. Soon after, I started skipping
school altogether in order to extend my socializing
hours. I would attend the first few classes and leave
the campus for lunch. Sometimes I would go home
and sometimes to a friend's house.

The majority of my friends were boys. It was

easier for me to fit in with them and I found it difficult to have girlfriends. I'm guessing that was because of the roles my parents played in my life. With my father being gone, I would always be looking for his replacement, and with the already damaged relationship with my mother, I would never feel comfortable around other girls. I never respected or liked them. During the days of cutting school and hanging out, I was also drinking heavily and smoking. This became my routine.

At home, I confined myself to my room, which was fine with my family. I didn't fit in with my mother and my two sisters, and in many ways, I resented them all. I read a lot, usually mystery novels—anything written by Agatha Christie, such as *And Then There Were None, Cat Among the Pigeons,* and *The Hollow.* Agatha took me to another world where the events leading to the ending of the novel were unpredictable. I enjoyed not knowing what was to come and would rush back into my room between meals and chores to find out who had killed whom and why. I was also a great fan of poetry and short stories and studied the works of Maya Angelou and Edgar Allan Poe. Maya wowed me with *I Know Why the Caged Bird Sings* and *Phenomenal Woman* and *And Still I Rise.* Maya gave my spirit strength with her mothering voice, while Edgar Allan Poe took me back to timeless and formal elegance in literature. I studied his techniques in such poems as "The Raven" and "Nevermore" and his short stories.

I discovered myself in books and in music. I listened to the radio, singing along, pretending. Imagining myself a star, I would reenact scenes from my favorite films and rehearse my acceptance speech to "The Academy" in front of the mirror. I spent time writing poetry and recording all my thoughts and pain in my journals, becoming increasingly introverted and an outsider in my own home.

Of all the Christmases I spent with my mother, one, when I was about fourteen, made the biggest impression on the rest of my life. From the day I came home after being raped, my mother began to tell anyone who would listen what an awful child I was. She told friends and family members that I was evil and on drugs. When the beatings were particularly vicious, I reached out to counselors and officials at my school. I showed up at school with bruises, lacerations, and even a sprained neck, but my mother had them all fooled. She lied to cover her actions and made me out to be the bad one, eventually succeeding in making everyone dislike me. Things had become inverted since we left St. Thomas, and now she was the good guy.

This particular Christmas, I left my room and walked slowly into the living room. There were maybe forty-five presents under the tree, and my little sisters were tearing away at their wrappings as my mother sat on the couch snapping pictures. I walked closer to the tree and my eyes began roaming around the base of it looking for my gifts. I wasn't expecting much but I was excited just the same. As I was looking, my sisters were yelling and screaming with joy to see the gifts from my mother as well as gifts sent from her family. My mother's family had always been split; her mother's side and her father's side. Once we moved to Florida, she disconnected from her mother's side and only acknowledged her father's family.

I stooped down and began kneeling so I could get a better view under the tree. I cleared away the mountains of torn wrapping paper and ribbons and pushed my sisters' gifts to one side. I continued to look, and as I did, no one said a word to me. No one even acknowledged my presence. I retreated from the Christmas tree once I realized there was nothing there for me. Not one thing. My mother had made everyone believe I was unworthy and no one in the family showed me love during the holiday. Of course her father's side of the family believed what she said; they had never known me. They had never loved me.

My heart sank into my stomach and it became a few degrees colder in the room. My mother could never have gotten away with this if my grandmother had been around. She had purposely disconnected me from my roots. She had brought me to this town to figuratively kill me off, and I would have to fight to stay alive.

I closed my bedroom door behind me and plowed into my mattress. At first, I began to cry. But then I received a phone call from a boy I liked that kids in the neighborhood called Bam-Bam. He was older than me, around nineteen years old, and had just moved to Florida from Queens, New York. I can't remember how we met, but I was glad we did. He was sweet to me and would always ask me how I was doing. He always wanted to know if I had a bad day and what was wrong.

I answered the phone to hear, "Hey, baby girl. Merry Christmas."

Smiling from ear to ear, I replied, "Hey, Bam, I'm not doing so good. I didn't get anything for Christmas and no one even spoke to me."

Bam-Bam seemed as disappointed as I was and said, "Don't worry, baby girl, I'll get you something. I'll have it for you when I see you again."

He made my day. I hung up the phone and lay in bed, feeling better. I replayed that conversation in my head over and over.

Over the next few years, things at home would continue to deteriorate. I decided to fight back. I told myself that the next time my mother put her hands on me, I would hit her back. I cannot recall exactly what the issue was on that day, but I do know that when my mother hit me, I kicked and punched back. I fought for my life that afternoon in the hallway of our apartment.

"Oh, you wanna fight?!" she screamed. "You wanna fight? You can't beat me! I will kill you!"

I believed her.

I didn't win that fight, and I realized I couldn't stay. I packed a few things, left my mother a note, and sneaked out of my first-story bedroom window. I was running away and had no intentions of ever coming back. I don't remember what was packed, but of the few belongings I was taking, my Wu-Tang Clan tape was my most treasured. It was my first hip hop tape and it would soon serve as the soundtrack to my first taste of voluntary freedom. I played that tape until the ribbon popped.

I had been on the streets for about two weeks, going from pillar to post, staying with friends and friends of friends. Everyone I knew was older than me and had their own apartment. I stayed with older boys, and I even stayed at an abandoned house of a guy who had been sent to prison. I was not alone, however. Charlene, my best friend, came along for the ride. She and I had never discussed what took place the night I was raped, but we still remained friends. We were soon met by some other runaway girls who frequented the area and knew the guy who owned the abandoned house.

I was homeless, underfed, and, on many days, dirty, with nowhere to take a shower. What I hadn't realized about this abandoned house was that it was in a crack-infested, prostitute-riddled neighborhood. I was so naive. One time I was standing on the corner with a couple of the girls from the house at the local liquor store asking for change to buy food and a stranger in a car invited us back to his place. We jumped into the car with a Jamaican stranger. I was eager to get something to eat and a place to shower. In retrospect, I realize he thought we were hookers, and he was looking for a good time at our expense. Fortunately, back at his place, his friend didn't want us, and we were consequently returned to the street corner where the guy had found us. Still, I would rather have lived in this abandoned building with no lights and no water, begging for food and money in the worst neighborhood in Tampa Bay, than go home.

It seems almost impossible to imagine now, but I lived on the street for close to a month. One Saturday night I was hanging out on the strip where there were teen clubs and places to eat, a movie theater and such. This was my first time in this part of town, and my first time hanging out like this. The night air felt cool and inviting on my face. We were all smiling and laughing and carefree. Charlene and I and the other girls from "our place" were all there together, acting like the kids we were. We weren't concerned about a thing. We didn't have any money or anywhere to go at the end of the night, but we were happy to be there among our peers. I was the happiest of all. I saw friends from school who I hadn't seen since I had run away, and they all let me know about the signs my mother had posted around the school and the neighborhood. I knew she would be looking for me, but I was shocked when I turned around to see her standing right behind me.

There was my mother, with her best friend in tow, side by side with a few members of the Tampa Bay Police Department. Her arms were folded tightly and I could see the look of ire on her face. She gave me the eye, and I knew my life would never be the same after this night. Suddenly her look changed from anger to concern and relief. It was a big act for the police. The police asked me why I left home, and I began to tell them about the beatings, about the time she hit me with a two-by-four wooden plank and hurt my neck, and about all the times I tried to tell the counselors at school, but she would come in and do the same thing she was doing now—lie and act.

"They can tell you," I said to the police, pointing to my friends. "They know."

My friends nodded in compliance. I knew this was my only chance. I had to convince the police that I was telling the truth. If I went home with my mother, I thought she would surely kill me.

"You're lying!" my mother shouted. "None of that ever happened!"

"Why are you lying like this?" her friend chimed in.

I don't blame her friend. She only had my mother's perspective to rely on and my mother did a good job painting this ugly portrait of me. She had turned the whole world against me, making them all think that I was on drugs and even that I was possessed by the devil. She told everyone I was a whore and that I had been having sex with all my guy friends, when nothing could have been farther from the truth. She defamed and degraded my character. I couldn't let her win on this night. I wouldn't. As I stood there in front of the police, I cried my heart out and begged them to believe me. I had become hysterical with desperation and began to hyperventilate. I was placed in the back of a squad car, two officers sat up front.

"Calm down, it's going to be okay," the officer on my right said. "We're here to help you."

He was there to *help* me? The very concept had become foreign to me. I felt as if no one had been on my side since we'd left St. Thomas. I had no one in Florida. There was no one to burst into the room and rescue me from her. Now it seemed as if someone might.

"Now, you know that if you don't go home, we'll have to take you to juvie," the officer said.

"I don't care," I said without hesitation. "Take me."

"You won't have any clean clothes there," he said. "And there's a uniform you'll have to wear every day. It's not as nice as the things you have on now. And the food is not so good, either, and the other kids there aren't nice like you are."

I did not flinch.

"Take me," I said. "Because if you send me back there, with her, I will kill her. If I don't, I'm certain that she will kill me. If you send me back, you'll just have to come get me again in the morning."

The look in the officer's eyes as they met mine—determined and defiant—gave me hope. The decision he made changed my life, yet again.

"Where's your father?" he asked.

I began to sob uncontrollably. "I don't know!"

"Well, what's his name?"

"Kenneth."

As soon as I blurted out the name of my father, the other officer jerked himself out of the car and went over to my mother. I could see him take out his pen and pad and begin to scribble feverishly. Within seconds, he was back in the driver's seat.

"Here's his name and his location," the officer said. "He's in Phoenix."

I was confused. I had no idea what my father would be doing in Arizona, since the last I'd heard he was in New York. Nonetheless, I felt relieved.

Before my sisters were born, my mother and I would run back and forth to New York from St. Thomas, chasing behind my father. When I was five, she moved us into a tiny fourth-floor studio apartment on the corner of Parsons Boulevard and Hillside Avenue in Jamaica, Queens. The hallways and stairwells were littered with homeless men who pissed on the walls and floors. On occasion, I would look outside one window in an apartment adjacent to ours and see a fat, naked man with a long grizzly beard, guzzling liquids and stuffing his face with leftover food from God knows where. I could look down the alley, between my building and his, and see the trash heap forming and the dog-sized rats running and ravaging through it. This was poverty at its finest, and I had been living in it because my mother was ever hopeful she could win my father back.

My father often came to see me. And on quite a few occasions, he would take me back to his house in Central Islip, Long Island. I loved it there. Leaf Avenue was a beautiful street, lined with towering oaks and two-story homes nestled on either side. At the end of this long, picture-perfect street was a church. And every hour on the hour, the church bell rang. To me, it was a constant reminder that I was safe and that God was there.

I was six around this time, and my father had two other daughters, Toni and Jennifer, from a previous marriage. Both Toni and Jennifer were more than a decade older than me. We played outside with the other neighborhood kids and they would try to teach me how to ride a bike, a two-wheeler, and my feet could barely reach the pedals. I stretched my limbs, trying to impress my big sisters. There was always a family of squirrels scurrying out of my way and up the trees, as if they knew I was new at this.

I remember so many things about that house and the neighborhood—the sounds, the smells, the people. The house next door had burned down and I thought to myself that our house must have been protected by God because it was unharmed. I remember catching fireflies or lightning bugs and putting them in glass jars, placing them beside our beds as we slept. They would be dead by morning and we replaced them with new ones every night. At the church at the end of our street, they served free lunch, and like clockwork, my sisters and I were there. Peanut butter and jelly sandwiches, milk and cookies. Those were good days for me. They were simple and I was safe.

My father had gotten my mother a job at B. Altman's department store in Manhattan in the men's department. He was a buyer at Bloomingdale's and had connections. My mother seemed happy. She did everything she could to be what she thought he needed. But I learned that my father was only tolerating her for my sake. This was obvious from the way she would beg him to stay when he visited our apartment and from the way she would become infuriated when all he wanted was to take me back to Long Island. During the days and weeks that I spent on Long Island, my father had no use for my mother because he had me. This made her furious. So one day, while my father was at work, my mother came to that perfect house, on that perfect block, in that perfect neighborhood, and took me away.

My father's mother, Merle, and his father, Edmund, and my sisters Toni and Jennifer watched as my mother snatched me up and drove off. I kicked and screamed and cried.

"Please don't make me go, please let me stay. Please! Please!" I cried. She slapped me and told me to shut up.

I reminisced to myself about those days as I sat in the back of the police car in Tampa, Florida. I was finally hopeful about something. I was looking forward to the possibility of seeing my father again.

"If we can track your father down, would you like to go live with him?" the officer asked.

I couldn't get the word *yes* out of my mouth fast enough. I said it twice to make sure it came out right.

"Yes! Yes!"

To my surprise, the officers worked on finding my father right then and there. They would not release me into the custody of my mother until they found him.

"We found your father. Now, tomorrow, we're all going to work on getting you to him," the officer said. "But for now, you'll have to go home with your mother. We've spoken to her and she's promised us that she will not lay a hand on you. Get there, get some rest, and get your things together. It looks like you'll be going to Phoenix!"

I smiled and cried all at the same time. Could this be true? Was I finally going to be leaving this hell? Was I really going to be safe and see my father for the first time in almost ten years? The deal was made. I would go home with my mother but not for long. I was Phoenix-bound.

Chapter Five

THE GREAT ESCAPE

I HAD MOVED TO SCOTTSDALE, a suburb of Phoenix, in January of 1994, and by the summer of 1995, I was ready to be on my own. My father lived well, and for the first time I was able to do things like go to the mall and actually shop. I was allowed to have friends and boyfriends over, and my dad was cool with everyone. I was free. There was no drama, except every once in a while I would get grounded for staying out past curfew. I didn't mind that because the punishment was deserved, and it never lasted too long. Not to mention that it was a lot better than being beaten.

All of my new friends came from wealthy households and were afforded the same privileges as me. We spent the scorching Arizona summers poolside at my house, barbecuing and listening to music. This was the life, and I was being spoiled.

But the good times didn't last for long. My father married his live-in girlfriend, Michelle, not long after I moved in. Less than a year later, my little sister Kaddie was born. Soon after that, my father's only son, Kenneth Jr., moved in with us from Maryland. My father had four other children, including Toni and Jennifer, who had all previously lived in different states. My father's mother, Merle, also lived at the house. It went from just me and my father to all of these people who, while they were related to me, were nonetheless strangers. My dad became stressed, and my stepmother had problems adjusting to being a new mother. I spent most of my time taking care of the newest addition to our family while Michelle worked her way through her issues. She would stay locked in the bedroom a lot, and I remember my father not handling it very well.

Soon there were screaming matches between Michelle and my father. His attitude began to change and he started treating me differently. I no longer had the freedom to do the things I had only just begun to enjoy, and even the simplest things, like getting my nails done, had now become an issue. Not surprisingly, money had become tight for my father, who was now responsible for a house full of people. The majority of my allowance was cut off and he was either unable or unwilling to do the things for me he had done when I'd first come to live with him. As my father and Michelle argued, my grandmother often got into the middle, frustrated with all of the fighting. It became too much for me. Regardless of how well I'd been living, I was still very fragile. Although I had become accustomed to the good life, I still carried traces of my old life with me.

During the summer after the eleventh grade, I shoved a few belongings into a Hefty bag, pocketed the $36.57 I had been saving, called a cab, and sneaked out of my bedroom window. I threw the bag over the six-foot-high concrete wall around our home and hoisted myself over it, being careful not to jump into the cacti that lined the other side of the wall. And just like that, I was gone again. The only plan I had was to get to a friend's apartment and to stay there for the night. I would figure out the rest in the morning.

It was such a crazy time for me I don't remember much about where I was and what I did as I moved from place to place with friends and even strangers. I do remember feeling the way I felt living with my mother in Tampa Bay—I would much rather have been on the streets as a derelict than to feel like I was in the way.

I had a boyfriend, Reggie, who was there for me. He had been on his own since he was sixteen, and his mother lived in New York, where he grew up. He and his mother had moved to Phoenix years before, but when she went back to New York, Reggie opted to stay. He was my high school love, and we spent every weekend and holiday break together. He didn't attend school and was essentially a hustler who lived in a bad neighborhood. I loved the excitement of knowing that I was with a "bad boy" and on many occasions would be both thrilled and terrified at hearing the gunshots outside. Around the time that I left home, Reggie's mom came to visit. I was instantly drawn to her. She was pretty and funny and treated both me and Reggie as if we were adults. I moved in with Reggie and his mother and her visit ended up being permanent.

After hanging out with her for a while, she and I became friends. She said she knew a way I could make money to support myself now that I was a woman out on my own. I looked up to her and was happy to take her advice. It's funny how I had so much admiration for her as a girl at sixteen, but I cannot remember her name now. Reggie's mom was a dancer at an all-nude exotic-dance club. Without asking for credentials, the managers allowed me to work there right away.

The room was dark, except for the stage, and was packed with patrons, their faces masked by cigarette smoke. As my turn approached, I was nervous. My heart was beating so fast and so loud that I could not hear the music over its thumping. I tried to tune it all out. I had to do it. I had to make it on my own. I went backstage to change into my outfit. It was a white bikini with a matching sheer, long robe. The outfit came highly recommended from Reggie's mom, since white glowed in the dark under the club's black lights. The song I chose for my very first dance was "Come Down" by Bush. The chorus blared from the speakers, *"I don't want to come back down from this cloud. / It's taken all this time to find out what I need."* I would dance to "Come Down" every night, as my first dance.

In the moments just before I made my debut, Yizette Santiago, my alter ego, was born. In order to get up on that stage every night and dance like I loved and meant it, I needed to put forth the persona of a fearless woman. So the scared little girl who felt unworthy, unattractive, and unwanted was gone. In her place was Yizette, a woman-child who was everything Karrine wanted to be—beautiful, sexy, confident, and independent.

When I took those first couple of steps that led to the stage and the spotlight hit my body, the crowd began to cheer. It is all a blank. I performed without thought, and movement came naturally to me. I got through it. I don't know what I did, or how I did it, but whatever I did was good enough for the crowd. They went wild. The next thing I remember is holding all of my money and making my way offstage. Reggie's mother was there, waiting with open arms.

"You did so good, baby girl," she said. "You were beautiful out there and they love you. Now hurry up, count your money and get back out there!"

And that's what I did—night after night. Every night I was pulling down a thousand dollars at the club. I was doing well, but my relationship with Reggie's mother turned sour. She was in her midthirties at the time, and it seemed as if her heyday was over. Mine, at seventeen, was just beginning. When she found out I was making substantially more money than her, she didn't like it. She began to take advantage of me and started charging me ridiculous amounts of rent and would even demand that I buy her things. Our friendly relationship turned into a jealous competition. And I was soon on the road again.

On December 26, 1995, I had been shopping at the mall, taking advantage of the post-Christmas sales and getting my nails done, when I received a call from an associate at another local strip club, an upscale place that most of the

NFL and NBA players in Phoenix frequented. I had already dated one or two players from the Arizona Cardinals and was enjoying my run as one of the most popular dancers in the city. I was a center attraction, a main feature at the club.

Your worth as a dancer is measured by how well you are able to hang upside down and spin from atop the ten-foot pole. It was equally important to know how to work the floor, gyrating and pulsating to the music in front of the customers who lined the stage. I was a champion in both areas. I racked up back-to-back table dances, where I would cuddle and caress the upper bodies of the patrons. Some were strangers, but many were regulars. I had mastered a table-dance trick, which was to turn the usual position into an unexpected handstand while wrapping my legs around the man's torso. It became my signature move. I was good at what I did and was paid accordingly.

One customer who paid very well exchanged numbers with me and called me one day to meet him and a friend for a private dance session at his friend's house. This was something I did often—private dances for the Arizona Cardinals players and bachelor parties. They sent a chauffeur to fetch me from the mall. I walked up to the brand-new, two-story home, which stood directly in the center of a welcoming cul-de-sac. I rang the doorbell. I could feel in my stomach how nervous I was about who would be answering the door. I really wasn't in the mood, but there was a lot of money at stake, which was always my motivation.

The door opened, and there stood Kool G Rap, an old-school rapper. I didn't know who he was. I only knew his name because that's how he was introduced. I wasn't that into rap and had never heard any of his music, and his face was not familiar. My first impression was that he was unattractive. I could barely stand to look at him, but he was charming and funny, and within no time, made me feel very comfortable. I cannot recall a lot of what happened that night, but I do know I never did dance for him. There was something about Kool G Rap, or G, as I started calling him, that made me feel protected. It may have been his two-hundred-and-eighty-pound frame or the reassuring bass in his voice. I'm not sure what it was, or if it was anything at all, but I stayed the night. He was twenty-seven at the time, and little did he know, I was only seventeen.

The very next morning, I was awakened by the sound of his booming voice, laced with his trademark lisp.

"Hey, what's your name again?" he asked me.

My eyes were barely open and I could hardly remember who or where I was. I gave him the name I had been using as a dancer, Yizette Santiago, since I was sixteen. It seemed plausible because I had the state ID, the Social Security card, and the W-2s to prove it, and they all stated that I was twenty-one years old. Once I got myself together, I realized that G was on the phone with an airline booking tickets to New York for later that night. For us.

"You're staying with me," he said. "You're going to be my wife." Though our union would not be legal because I was a minor and not truthfully Yizette Santiago, from that day on, I was his wife in every way. But there was something else he wanted. He begged me, even ordered me, to call him "Daddy." I refused over and over again. I was strong then. I had been on my own for a while, making my own money. It was difficult for me to let anyone tell me what to do and even more difficult for me to give someone a title of authority. But somehow, some way, I finally broke down and said it. It drove him wild.

Once we hit New York, we found ourselves at his manager, Chuck's, Upper East Side Manhattan apartment making love. It was the dead of winter and the room was ice-cold. The sounds of the city swirled below; the blaring horns of taxicabs and the ear-piercing whistles of people trying to catch them. There was heavy snow on the ground and I could hear the tires of the cars below grinding into it. I missed this city and there was nothing sweeter than having sex in it. Just as he was close to orgasm, I yelled out, "Fuck me, Daddy!" and the look in his eyes told it all. He was hooked.

Two weeks later, we were back in Arizona. We lived in a posh, new neighborhood in a twenty-five-hundred-square-foot, four-bedroom house on about an acre of land. The first and second stories were connected by a grand spiraling staircase and the house was blessed with skylights throughout. It wasn't as large as the mansions I had become accustomed to while dating and sometimes living with professional athletes, but it was beautiful. I was beginning to become used to my new home and all of the rules that G insisted upon. He had a definite way of doing things, and most importantly, a definite way that he wanted me to do things. We bumped heads almost immediately.

The first time G hit me, I should have left him. He had been on the phone with another woman. While he spoke on the handset downstairs I went upstairs and unplugged the base from the wall. I found his behavior disrespectful and had had enough. It wasn't the first time I'd caught him talking to other women; sometimes he'd talk to them all day and he didn't seem to care if I knew or not. He'd be on the phone for hours on end, with woman after woman, without saying a word to me. Yet I was expected to cook four times a day, clean the entire house, and do the laundry. On the day I disconnected his call, I heard his heavy footsteps storming up the staircase. I had a smirk on my face, expecting a bit of confrontation and a quick resolve, but that is not what he had in mind. As I sat on the edge of the bed waiting for the argument, which I was sure I would win, he entered the room from my right, stood directly in front of me, and with his left hand slapped me off the bed and onto the floor. It hadn't been the first time I had been hit—from my mother, to boyfriends in high school, and even a recent boyfriend before I met G. As a matter of fact, I had come to expect it.

So there we were. I was the wife of a man who insisted I call him Daddy, who chastised me as if he were my real daddy, who gave me the rules and boundaries I'd longed for and the order and responsibility I had been lacking, all the while ruling over me with an iron fist, literally. From that first slap to the face, I was subservient, which was just the way he wanted me.

I should have left; I should have grabbed my things and headed out of the door. After all, I barely knew him and had been on my own before. But I was tired of running. I had nowhere else to go. My father had already told me that I could never come back to his house. That was the rule for all of his children. Once you're out, you may never come back, no matter what. I didn't want to be a stripper anymore. I'd grown tired of the late nights and gawking men, and had been desperate for a way out. G gave me that out. He gave me a home, and soon his family became my family. His sister and brother became my own, and I spoke to his mother, who I'd begun to call "Mom," every day. I hadn't spoken to my own mother in years. Admittedly, I stayed with G for all the wrong reasons, and our relationship would only go from bad to worse.

G did, however, shower me with gifts and trips during the first few months of our relationship. I was only a teenager and hadn't learned a lot about the finer things in life. While I had been around some of the wealthiest men in the city, I was still very much a tomboy. Since high school, I had been dressing in oversize boys' clothes and never left home wearing anything but sneakers and toting a backpack. I was not as worldly as I would have liked to believe I was, and G was the first to open that door for me. He taught me about perfumes and purses, changing my habit of wearing his cologne to having the best of Chanel and Versace pure perfumes, and switching my dirty backpack with the latest Dooney & Bourke and Coach bags. He educated me on the cut, color, and clarity of diamonds and the most precious of stones. We ate well every day. Lobster tails, colossal shrimp, and the choicest cuts of beef and lamb. We drank Cristal champagne with our orange juice in the morning and all throughout the day. I was made to ditch my oversize jeans and tees for dresses and skirt ensembles. G taught me a lot about being a woman, but he taught me to be an unsure and abused one, too.

Amid all of the perks of being with one of the most

renowned pioneers of rap were a number of disadvantages and dangers. I was not allowed to wear makeup and was not allowed to do anything too drastic to my hair. All of my dresses and skirts, though feminine, had to be loose-fitting and past my knee. I was also not allowed to talk to any of my friends on the phone, and if I did, he would become angry and even jealous because I was giving attention to someone other than him. The beatings continued and worsened as time went on.

Once, I prepared a lunch of shrimp and linguine and made the horrible mistake of leaving the tails on the shrimp. In my mind, that's the way they had always been served to me in restaurants, and I saw no harm in offering the shrimp to him in this manner, along with a knife to remove the tails. I served G his favorite dish and proudly retreated to the kitchen with a slight smile on my face. The rule was to always serve him first and then go back and serve myself. But as I loaded pasta onto my plate, G let out one of his many taunts to which I had become so accustomed.

"Yo, what the fuck is the matter with you?! Who the fuck leaves tails on fucking shrimp?!"

He ordered me to cut the tails off the shrimp and remake his plate. Trembling and praying that I would do it right this time, I scraped the unused portion of his lunch back into the pot and began to remove the tails from the shrimp before re-serving him on a new plate. I was sure that I had gotten it right this time and would be spared his wrath. Again he yelled and called me stupid and worthless. I didn't understand; I had done what he asked.

As I stood in the kitchen, clutching my nervous stomach, he rose from his seat and walked toward me with his plate in hand. He rested his plate next to me on the counter with his right hand, and just as soon as he did, he slapped me with his left.

"Stupid fucking bitch! What the fuck is wrong with you?!" he screamed over me as I picked myself up off the floor. I still didn't understand, not even after he explained.

When he received the first plate, for some reason, he hadn't seen the tails on the shrimp before he began eating them. Once he noticed the scaly crunching in his mouth, he spit the food back onto the plate. When I went to make him a fresh plate, I had scraped the food from his plate into the pot, to keep it warm, while I picked all the shrimp out to remove their tails. I then re-served him the same linguine and the shrimp he had spit out. Any simple mistake would set him off. It didn't take much.

Chapter Six

THE BEGINNING OF THE END

WITHIN THE FIRST FOUR MONTHS of my relationship with G, I had lost forty pounds and weighed a pitiful ninety-six pounds. The stress of the physical and verbal abuse had taken a toll on my body and spirit. G called me skinny and ugly, and had no problem telling me how unattractive I was to him since the weight loss. Life at our house was torture. It was common to see me with bruises up and down my body. His ex-girlfriend would come by the house, and even though she hated me, she'd sometimes cry at the sight of my emaciated, bruised, and swollen body. Still, I protected him.

On one occasion, we were playing a video game in the living room. He was sitting on one couch and I was on the other. During the game, he began to call me a stupid bitch. G had a way of looking at me with disgust that turned my stomach, and sometimes I would just throw up at the outset of an argument. He gave me the look, and at that moment I tried to be brave and fight back. I wanted to be tough, just as he had been to me. I wanted to let him know that I, too, was a force to be reckoned with, but all I could do was throw the game controller at him. It landed lightly on his lap, but it wouldn't have mattered if it hadn't hit him at all. That I showed any kind of mutiny was reason enough for what happened next.

Within seconds, he rose from his seat and punched me in my right side. It must have been a kidney punch, the type that boxers receive, because my body crumpled to the floor. I was unable to stretch out. My organs had shut down and I couldn't breathe. I was suffocating, and if he had hit me one more time, I feared I would die. I tried to speak, but I couldn't.

I was barely able to say the words, "I can't breathe."

All of a sudden, as he stood over me with his balled fists, his anger turned to fright. He picked my stiff body up off the floor and tried to administer CPR, then opened the front door and began to yell into the street for help.

I could hear him screaming, "Oh my God, help me!" and in my waning consciousness, I began to feel sorry for him and less concerned about me.

One of our neighbors was a nurse, and she administered CPR. The ambulance arrived a few minutes later. Once I arrived at the hospital, the nurses and doctors asked me how I had cracked my ribs.

G answered for me: "She was running and tripped over the chair."

When the nurse was alone with me, she inspected my

bruised side. I knew she did not believe G's version of what happened, especially because there was evidence of an imprint of his fist. But I backed up his story. I protected my Daddy. It was as if I suffered from a case of Stockholm syndrome during which the hostage somehow becomes enamored with the captor, and even begins to identify with the captor, as a defense mechanism born out of fear of violence. Even the smallest acts of kindness by the captor are magnified. These symptoms occur under tremendous emotional and often physical duress. This behavior is considered a common survival strategy for victims of interpersonal abuse and has been observed in battered spouses and abused children. Though I needed to get out of this dangerous, extremely unhealthy relationship, I sided with G and returned to that house.

Once we returned home from the hospital, I found it hard to even walk. I turned on the water in our glassed-in shower as he lit the fire in the adjacent double-sided fireplace. Sharp pains ran all through my body, and as I stood under the water, I began to cry as I realized that I could not raise my hands to wash myself. I was broken and couldn't even get myself clean. G heard my sobs, and in his charming way, he disrobed and joined me in the shower. He hurt me and then made it all better as he washed me gently and showered me with kisses and repeatedly whispered, "I love you."

Still, the abuse continued. I was not allowed to check the mailbox after a while because he thought I was seeing someone around the corner, where the community mailboxes were located. I was also not allowed to learn how to drive, to hold a job, or to further my education, beyond receiving my GED. On the few occasions when I got employment at the local mall, he called my job constantly, and I frequently called home, feeling guilty for leaving him alone. It wasn't unusual for him to say, "I need you. Come home." It was common for me to run back to him rather than moving toward gaining my independence.

One day I woke up and decided I didn't want to live like this anymore. In fact, I didn't want to live. I took a full bottle of prescription painkillers and was rushed to the hospital, where they made me drink charcoal to neutralize the effects of the medicine. There were times when I locked myself in a closet with G's gun, playing with its barrel and trigger, wanting to shoot myself, hesitating only because I was afraid of the pain. I wanted out of my life, one way or the other.

Living with one of hip hop's pioneers, I started to get lost in the new world of hip hop and the glorious videos accompanying the latest hot singles. I looked enviously at the women in these videos, their bodies perfectly voluptuous while mine was gaunt and disgusting. Their faces were all made up, and mine was plain, with only the shine of lip balm on my lips. Their clothes were tight-fitting, and mine hung loosely from my sticklike frame. I wanted to be there, wherever they were. It was my greatest wish, to be beautiful and strong and free.

G would become very upset with me if I liked someone else's music too much. He would take another artist's success as a reminder of his own increasing irrelevance. Kool G Rap began and sustained his career in the eighties and into the early nineties. He has been dubbed one of hip hop's most revered pioneers, yet he has not been as successful or recognized as many of his counterparts. It is easy for some to remember Big Daddy Kane, Biz Markie, and Rakim, artists who enjoyed more mainstream success. But G stayed more underground, rarely finding himself on MTV, as his protégé Nas had. When we were together, it appeared that his peers and even his students would surpass him. His most popular singles like "Streets of New York," "Ill Street Blues," and "Road to the Riches" are rarely ever heard outside of the East Coast's tristate area. He was big at a time when there was no SoundScan, the tool that is used to track record sales. He never had the privilege of knowing just how many records he had sold, whereas his younger counterparts were going platinum-plus in the mid- to late nineties. This sense of failure or incompletion, I believe, is what fueled G's rage at times, and I would find myself watching videos when he wasn't around so I would not make him angry while I was dreaming of a new life.

For now, I would remain in the nightmare called my life. There were multiple abortions and miscarriages. I'd reached the end of my rope. I staggered to the bathroom and, after locking the door behind me, fell to my knees and continued to cry over the toilet. I prayed to God to save me. I begged Him to give me a child who would be strong enough to live inside me and endure the abuse. I promised Him that if He would answer my prayer, it would be my motivation to leave. My existence alone was not enough. I needed another reason to save my life. I knew that having a child would bring me back to health and give me the strength to live without G. I prayed to God for that chance. Later that night, my son was conceived.

Before too long, G and I were at it again. I can't remember what the fight was about, but in the middle of him kicking me out of the house yet again, I blurted, "I'm pregnant!" and his response was typical.

"Bitch, I don't care. Get out!" So I did.

I stayed with friends for the next two weeks until G allowed me to come back home. I was made to sleep in the guest room, on the floor, with just one blanket and one pillow. I was not allowed in the master suite at any time during the day unless I had been summoned to have sex with him. It was mostly oral sex. He called it my "apology." G would stroke the back of my head and say things like "That's right, show Daddy how sorry you are. Apologize to your Daddy. Suck Daddy's dick and Daddy won't be mad at you no more. That's what a good girl is supposed to do."

He made me perform on him for up to two hours at a time. On one occasion, it went on so long, my nose bled. It was supposed to be my way of taking responsibility for whatever I had done to make him so angry. It was always my fault, and I was always made to apologize.

The pregnancy proved to be a difficult one. I was constantly sick and unable to stand even the sight of certain foods, especially meat. I was unable to keep anything down and continued to be underweight at a time when I should have been putting on weight from the baby's growth inside of me. I was also severely anemic and found it hard to get out of bed to shower, much less to perform the daily household chores. Still, I was made to cook and clean and carry on as if everything were the same. The rule was that G should never have to cook his own meals or do anything else around the house as long as there was a woman living with him.

One day, we were in the midst of yet another battle when he had ordered me to leave the house. He packed up most of my things and had them waiting by the door. I was about three months pregnant at this time, and it was the middle of the night.

I was crying and shaking, screaming out to him, "I have nowhere to go! Where will I go?! It's two in the morning!"

His answer was for me to go to a shelter. So, at his command, I thumbed through the Yellow Pages and found a shelter with an open bed that would pick me up from the house. I continued to cry and beg for him to just let me sleep there, even offering to go back to the guest room and sleep on the floor. He denied me. Yet, while I was waiting for the shelter to come get me, G had one more order to place and that was for me to make him a steak. So I stood there, making his steak, crying and shaking, still begging to stay. I became nauseous and began cooking and throwing up simultaneously. G's concern was not for my health, or for the health of his unborn child, but that his steak would not be burned. Just a few moments after I served him his perfectly cooked steak, my ride was at the door. I was then hauled off to the homeless shelter in the seediest section of downtown Phoenix, my designer bags filled with designer clothes and shoes.

There were about ten other women in the room to which I was assigned. There was only one shower, where up to five women could bathe at a time, with no curtain to shield their bodies from anyone walking by. I had only twenty cents in my purse and managed to borrow a nickel from one of the homeless women who was a permanent resident of the shelter. With the twenty-five cents, I called one of my best friends, Cecily, and she took me home with her the morning after I arrived at the shelter. I was lucky. I had somewhere to go. The other women at the shelter had nothing. There was so much despair and hopelessness around me. I could feel the hopelessness.

Eventually, I returned home to G and to all of the awful things that came with living in his house. Throughout the rest of my pregnancy, the abuse continued. During my fourth month, it became almost physically impossible for me to have sex. It was extremely painful and would also make me nauseous. Still, that was of no concern to G, and on many occasions we had sex even when I didn't want to, and he ignored my tears as I cried through each episode. I can remember him yelling at me after sex because the crying made it difficult for him to reach orgasm. Again I was being a bad girl. As a result, oral sex became more prevalent in our relationship. My mouth and neck were in constant pain. There was no way I could ever refuse him. It got to the point where just the smell of his skin would make me throw up, and I could not serve him anymore without making him feel unloved and unwanted. G would make me pay over and over again.

In my seventh month of pregnancy, G had been called away to New York for work. Not long after his arrival in the city, I was awakened by a call from one of his friends. G had had a grand mal seizure in the limo on the way from the airport. It wasn't his first seizure; the problem began many years before I met him. G had told me that he had a preexisting condition that required brain surgery. He also mentioned that on another occasion he had been rushed to the hospital after he had been sniffing cocaine with his friend, singer Bobby Brown. From what I'd been told, G had not been doing any drugs at the time of his seizure in the limo. He told me that the last time he did cocaine was actually just a few weeks after we met. The cocaine was given to him by the assistant of one of my NFL friends, a linebacker with whom G had also become friends, not knowing of my past sexual relationship with the athlete.

Several hours after I received the phone call about G's seizure, I got on a flight and was in upstate New York to check G out of the hospital. His neck was sore and he had bitten his tongue, which was swollen and tender. It softened my heart to see him so fragile. It was the first time I had ever seen him actually need me. I held his hand and helped him out of bed; I helped him get dressed and put on his shoes. We walked out of there together, and anything that had gone wrong in our relationship was no longer a factor.

Over the next two weeks, G and I stayed with his mother, Hanyifah, in the South Ozone Park section of Queens, New York. The house was a disaster. There were roaches everywhere and everything was falling apart. I'd lived in less modern, less desirable places during my life, but I had never seen anyone living in this type of shambles. I was shocked, thinking about how well G and I lived in comparison to his own mother. Still, I loved being there with his mother and the rest of his family. G's mother and I slept in the same bed. She would place her hands on my stomach and feel my son moving. She would cry and talk to him in her sweet, tiny voice. G was away from the house in the recording studio for most of our days there, so his mother and I lay in bed, watching *The Young and the Restless,* game shows, and talk shows. She was extremely ill and frequently had to use a wheelchair to get around. She needed help getting out of bed and down the stairs. She had many pains in her life, but her son and our unborn baby brought her renewed joy.

For the most part, things were going well at this time. G and I had not fought in a while and were getting along. But the peace in our lives was only temporary. One day while G and I showered together, he said, "I think we need another woman to take your place, since you can't fuck properly." I was appalled. The look on his face was almost innocent, as if he saw no wrong in what he had just told his pregnant wife. I blew up and jumped out of the shower. He followed me around the house as I yelled and he yelled back. I couldn't understand. He made it seem as if it was all my fault and that because of me, he had to have another woman. The fight continued downstairs, where his mother sat in her wheelchair.

"What the hell is going on?" she asked, in as loud a voice as she could muster.

She worked herself out of her chair and began to confront her son. I had worked myself into hyperventilation and severe stomach cramps. Without much warning, I collapsed, and his poor, sick mother tried her best to hold me up when she herself should have been in her wheelchair. G, again, was not concerned about either of us and stormed out of the house. I could never win with him, and no matter how much wrong he had done, his mother would never completely side against her son. How could she? What's more, his mother needed G more than I did. He was the only breadwinner in the family and everyone depended on him for support.

G suffered another seizure once we returned to Arizona. He had stopped taking the Tegretol that had been prescribed by his doctor to help control his seizures. He said that taking the medicine made him feel like less of a man. During the first week of January 1998, his seizures returned. I was nine months pregnant at the time. G had been in the hallway bathroom, and while he was sitting on the toilet, the seizure hit. I heard him falling off the toilet and shaking against the tub. I jumped out of bed and ran to his side. His eyes were rolled back in his head and his tongue was hanging out and locked between his teeth. I quickly called 911, grabbed his Tegretol bottle, called his mother, and unlocked the front door. I then ran back to wipe his ass, flush the toilet, and pull up his boxers so he would not be embarrassed when the ambulance arrived. Once they had him on a gurney, I got dressed and grabbed a set of clean clothes for him to wear when he left the hospital to return home. All of this was done in a matter of minutes. No matter the abuse and the trauma I suffered on his watch, I still took care of him.

Over the next two weeks, I nursed G back to health. He

had a cocktail of medicines which had to be administered every three hours or so. I made sure he took all of them on time, even in the middle of the night. I would set my alarm clock to wake me up at eleven at night, and at two and five in the morning. I ignored my pregnancy needs at the time to be sure to get him well. I would also rub his neck and shoulders every few hours, for they had been severely injured during his seizure. Soon G fully recovered, and within days of his recovery, we were back in the hospital to welcome our baby boy.

On January 17, 1998, I went into labor. On that day, I stayed home and counted my contractions. By the next morning, the pain was unbelievable, so we checked into the Thunderbird Samaritan Hospital. G stayed with me every second. He supported me fully and was the charming and loving man I knew him to be from time to time. I was just nineteen years old, and for the next twenty-four hours, I continued to be overwhelmed with pain, until finally, fifty-one hours into my labor, my son was born. After almost three full days and the legal limit of five epidurals, I was exhausted. G seemed to be excited and jumped around the room taking pictures. I couldn't physically feel the moment that my son was born, but as I pushed, I focused on G's face as he winked at me to check to see if I was all right. I winked back as a signal that everything was just fine. Indeed, the most amazing thing was happening to me. As my son was being delivered from my body, the love I thought I felt for G automatically transferred to the new man in my life. And from that moment at 12:11 on the afternoon of January 19, 1998, I no longer loved Kool G Rap.

Chapter Seven

BREAKING AWAY

Over the next year, my interest in being with G had gone from little to none. I became enamored with my little boy. My days and nights were devoted to him. Being a mother came naturally to me after so much practice with my sisters. I was no longer cooking and cleaning constantly at G's command. After the baby was born, I no longer cared that much about G's needs, wants, and demands. We were, however, a family, and to strangers, we must have looked picture-perfect.

On our first night home from the hospital, the baby found it hard to get to sleep. He was about three days old. As he lay in his bassinette next to our bed, he screamed for almost an hour. When I tried to console my son, G forbade it, saying he would be spoiled.

I fought my maternal instinct for a while, but eventually grabbed my son and brought him to bed with me. From that night on, I slept with my back turned to G and with the baby nestled tightly in my arms, against my heart, and the sound of its beating would soothe the baby all night long.

It became evident that G had no paternal instinct. He once said he wanted a baby just to see what he could make. Once he saw him, his interest quickly faded. One night I placed the baby in bed between us for a few moments as I sat up to drink a glass of water I'd left on my nightstand. G rolled over onto the baby and had begun to smother him with his arm. I aggressively pushed G off my son. As time went on, I began to feel as if I had to choose between my son and his father. G had a way of pouting angrily. He sucked his teeth and blinked his eyes excessively. It was a silent intimidation, and one day he even admitted to me that he had become jealous of our son and the attention I showered on him. The baby took all of my time and energy. From the moment he was born, his needs superseded everyone's, especially G's. In general, I knew it was normal for fathers to feel this way, but when it came to G and his pattern of behavior, there was no telling what shape his jealousy would take and how much further it would erode our relationship. On February 8, 1998, my son was twenty days old. I was holding him while going about my business around the house. I had been expressing my milk and making bottles, which would usually take hours out of my day. G asked me to make his lunch, and I tried to reason with him that there just wasn't enough time and that maybe he should make his own food for a change.

With that angry pout and look of disgust on his face, he said, "Well, I'm going to get somebody in here to do all the shit you can't do."

"Who . . . who are you gonna get?!" I shot back angrily.

Back and forth we went. He was taunting me about finding a replacement for me, since our son was taking up so much of my time. Then, without warning, as I stood holding Naiim, G spat in my face. I, surprisingly, spat back in his. Over and over we exchanged spit until finally he placed his huge hands over my entire face, gripping tightly, and pushed me down to the ground, then finished me off with a slap to the face. My nose began to bleed. I looked down at my son. He cried while I continued to hold him, and his face was covered with my blood. This would be the first and only time I had G arrested for domestic violence.

We lived in a suburb of Phoenix called Glendale, and the police department had become very familiar with our house on Morning Dove Drive. They were called out at least twice a month, and once I was arrested for defacing property when I broke a glass in the kitchen during a fight. G had done this out of spite and malice. I stood alone in the kitchen as he stood in the living room. As soon as the glass was broken, he called the police. The rule was that if the police had been called to a residence twice in one night, someone had to be arrested. G knew this, and on that night he made the second call.

The impact of seeing my newborn son with a blood-covered face let me know the time to go was near. All I needed was money. Although G and I had enjoyed the financial benefits of his music career at the start of our relationship, the money quickly dried up. Hip hop was growing by leaps and bounds, and consequently, the competition was steep. G, like most, constantly strove to find his place as an artist, but that also meant we often did not have enough money to cover our basic living expenses, let alone spend freely.

For the next six months, I waited for the right time. G continued to have serious money issues, but there was new money on its way since he had recently signed an independent record contract. In the meantime, G and I continued to fight. One night we were at it as usual. I don't remember exactly when this occurred, but my son had just begun to learn how to stand. He had been asleep in his playpen in our bedroom when the argument G and I were having got loud. I could feel myself getting stronger as time went on. When he spit, I would spit back. When he screamed, so would I. I was nearing my breaking point, and on this night, as I saw his hands ball up in preparation to strike me, I leaped at him with the intention to strike first. I knew I could never hurt him physically, but it was the principle. As I lunged, I proved to be too slow as he raised his fist and punched me in the mouth.

I fell to the floor, face-first, and automatically checked for all of my teeth. They were all in place, but my lip was split and bleeding. I was wearing one of G's white T-shirts, which I instantly used as a makeshift bandage. I got up from the floor, grabbed the phone, and raced to the hall bathroom, locking myself in. He stood at the door, whimpering and begging for me not to call the police again. He was scared, almost in tears, and I was in shock. It was the first time he had scarred my face, and I cried as I looked at the hideous results. I did not call the police that night. I called his mother in New York. After explaining the incident to her, I opened the door and handed him the phone. I was screaming and crying, "You busted my face . . ." While he was on the phone, I found myself wandering the street in his bloody T-shirt, screaming at the top of my lungs. It was late, maybe after eleven at night. Before anyone could see me, he ran out, threw me over his shoulder, and placed an ice pack on my lip.

A few months later, G packed his bags and was on his way to the East Coast for a promotional tour to support his new independent album, *Roots of Evil*. About a week or so before he was to leave, I made the decision to have my breasts augmented to reverse the effects of breast-feeding my son; one had significantly changed and was very different from the other. G would tell me they were fine, but I knew it was lie. By this time I had lost all the weight I gained during my pregnancy. I was 96 pounds before getting pregnant and 140 pounds after giving birth. By the time my son was six months old, I was back down to about 100 pounds.

I was determined to leave G very soon and was slowly preparing myself. I knew that with no formal education or training of any kind, I would have to resort to stripping to take care of my son and me. G showed little interest in supporting his two oldest children, one of whom suffers with cerebral palsy. I knew what he was capable of (or not capable of), but I also knew what I was capable of. I was getting stronger and would be leaving for good.

The day G left for the promotional tour was the same day that I had my surgery. He took me to the doctor and picked me up after the procedure. If he hadn't been so preoccupied with his tour at the time, I never would have been able to get away with having the surgery. As soon as we got to the house, G was on his way to the airport. He assigned one of his friends to stay with me and the baby since I was still feeling the effects of the anesthesia.

The baby remained in the bed with me for the first two weeks as I recuperated. Under heavy medication, I managed to make bottles and change diapers. Initially, not having G around was a good thing. It gave me the freedom I needed to heal and grow into the woman I wanted to be, without him.

During this time, not only did I get my body back in order, but I also learned how to drive and acquired a driver's license. I bought new clothes to fit my new body and experimented with makeup and different hairstyles and colors. I also began to experiment with music. One of the rules of G's house was that I was not allowed to listen to the music of other male artists. He would get jealous and assume that I wanted to be with that person. On one occasion, earlier in our relationship, I had become a fan of a song that Boyz II Men performed for the soundtrack of the movie *Soul Food*. The song was a sweet ode to mothers, and I would listen to it and imagine that my son (not yet conceived) would feel that way about me. However, G saw it another way. He forbade me to listen to that song, insinuating that I would want to have an affair with at least one of the members of Boyz II Men.

He was the same way about a lot of other artists. So,

when he left, I went hip hop crazy. At this time I discovered DMX, Nas, AZ, and The Firm. It's also when I began to see the genius in Jay-Z, Biggie, and Tupac. I began to feel like Lauryn Hill knew my pain during my separation with G, and like she was a big sister. She made me stronger with her words. Her album *The Miseducation of Lauryn Hill* spoke to me and helped build me back up to where I was before I knew G. I listened to hip hop's men talk about "bad bitches," and I wanted to be one. They gave me a vision to strive for. Soon I was ready and waited for G to return so I could finally leave. But G had one more trick up his sleeve.

The time flew. Without my realizing it, G had been gone for three months. He stopped sending money for food and bills. The baby began to run out of diapers and formula. G had cleaned out our accounts, moved in, unbeknownst to me, with an ex-girlfriend in New York, and had given her all the money from our accounts. He stopped taking my calls, and no matter how much I begged for assistance, he would not comply. One night I had a dream. I called his name, in my dream, begging him to come home with me, but he turned his back and walked toward another woman. That's how I knew. I asked him if he was with someone and he denied it. I asked, quietly, for him to tell me and we would work it out. Still, he denied me. I began my own investigation, calling the girlfriend of one of his best friends in New Jersey, and before long, I had my answers. I called G at her house at one in the morning.

"Hi, Ashley, this is Yizette. Can I speak to G, please?"

He got on the phone and I asked him, "Why didn't you tell me? I asked you and you lied to me." I asked him to please send some money for us and we would talk about everything else when he returned.

His response was typical of the man I had known: "Fuck you, you stupid bitch! I don't give a fuck! I'm not sending you shit! You'll just have to suffer."

On and on, he went, and with every word, my strength diminished. Everything was my fault again, and I would be made to pay. Eventually, a friend of G's came over and brought some money for food and expenses. Because of the stress, I continued to lose weight. By the time G made it back, my son was a year old. He had missed his first birthday, his first step, and his first word—"Mommy."

True to form, G brought gifts when he arrived home from his escapades. Yet when our son saw his face and heard his voice, Naiim cried. Anytime G entered the room, my son cried. We both knew that our relationship was over. He decided that he would give me the money I needed to leave—thirty-five hundred dollars. That would have been enough to get an apartment and a car. I waited for him to give me the money he'd promised, during which time G continued to torture me. He moved his ex, who hated me, into the house. Although there were two empty bedrooms upstairs, she and their son slept on the living-room floor, and I was trapped upstairs unless I wanted some sort of confrontation. She and G had never gotten along, until right then, which was just for his convenience and spitefulness. All of a sudden they were the best of friends, hanging out all day, laughing and carrying on. I was an outsider in my own home and had to sneak around to avoid confrontations with either or both of them.

G was not beating me physically at this time, but inside, I was bruised and battered. He also never missed a moment to tell me how ugly and skinny I was, how he was disgusted just looking at me. G spent hours upon hours on the phone with his girlfriend in New York, Ashley. The phone and other bills of the household were in my name and all I wanted to do was to cut everything off, but I knew I would only be asking for more problems if I did. My strategy was to get through and get out.

I waited three long weeks for the thirty-five hundred dollars. In the end, all he gave me was a thousand. Toward the end of the three-week period, I began to realize that he was never going to give me what I needed in order to leave. He needed me to need him, even if he wanted nothing to do with me. He enjoyed seeing my bony frame and lifeless eyes because he knew that not only was he the reason for my state, he also controlled it. Just as he had explained why he'd wanted a child—just to see what he could create—so now he wanted to see what he could destroy. I began to pack. Many of my belongings I would leave behind, but I packed most of the baby's things. Anything big or heavy would have to be left behind. I had eight hundred dollars left after buying luggage and basic necessities.

I hid my bags and made no references to my leaving. G had gotten me an apartment in the same neighborhood we lived in, which was about an hour away from the city. I had no car and no resources; I could not be staying there.

I hit the wall the day G was on the phone in our loft with Ashley for more than six hours and finally went to bed around two in the morning. I had already called a friend of mine who worked for an airline on G's cell phone, being sure to erase the number after I hung up. I lay in bed with my son, pretending to be asleep. I waited for the sound of the phone hanging up. Finally, he threw himself into bed, and within minutes, began to snore. I slid out of bed, called my friend from the loft phone, and placed my bags at the door. I snuggled my one-year-old son in his winter coat as he slept. Without a hitch, my son and I quietly walked out and closed the door on a painful chapter. It was January 1999, and I was finally leaving Kool G Rap for good.

Chapter Eight

FIRE AND ICE

As I rode away from the home G and I had shared for the past three years, my heart seemed to sink into my stomach. I refused to look back, afraid I would lose my nerve. That night my son and I slept over at my friend's house, and early the next morning he put us on an airplane to Los Angeles.

G's former manager, Chuck, had made arrangements for us to stay for a week at his apartment in Studio City, a suburb of Los Angeles, while he vacationed in Hawaii. Chuck had recently moved to L.A. and was now the head of Artists and Repertoire for Dr. Dre's Aftermath Records. Chuck and I had stayed in touch, unbeknownst to G, and he had been fully aware of the relationship troubles from the very beginning. He had even stayed with G and me at our home for the first few months of our relationship. I was relieved to have somewhere else to go, even if only for a little while.

Chuck was waiting at baggage claim when Naiim and I arrived at Burbank Airport. I tried to make eye contact with him, yet he kept sweeping over me with his eyes. Finally, I called his name, and as his eyes settled upon me, they became frozen in disbelief. He had not recognized me for my extremely thin, ninety-five-pound frame. My eyes were sunken in, with dark circles around them, and my rib cage clearly showed through my clothes. I dove into his arms and began to cry with relief.

Chuck soon got us settled in his apartment, making sure that we had food to eat and that I was acquainted with the property-pool, laundry room, and what not. The purpose for this weeklong trip to Los Angeles was for me to collect my thoughts and get myself together. I had a lot to think about. There were custody and child-support issues to figure out. I also needed to have a plan for my immediate future. I needed to find a way to buy a car and go to school so I could get a job to support myself and my son. I used that week in Los Angeles to recuperate in order to go back to Phoenix stronger.

On one of my last nights in Los Angeles, Chuck saw to it that one of his friends took me out for a night on the town. I was feeling extremely awkward but still very excited to be going out. This was the first time that I would be introduced to the infamous Sunset Strip and the House of Blues. I remember walking around and the response of the men who walked past me. They would grab my arms and hands and ask me to dance. I was flattered, but still unsure of myself, so I would decline.

The night was coming to a close and I began to search for Chuck's friends. During my search, I was stopped by yet another man, who quickly introduced himself as Marquis from the notorious 2 Live Crew. We had a brief exchange and he wrote his phone number on a napkin as I promised to call him the next day. As I walked away, my eyes wandered about and soon became fixated on a man, surrounded by women. He stood in the shadows and all I could make out was his fedora and the ringlets of hair which dangled from under it. He also carried a walking stick, and from what I could tell, was very well dressed in a well-tailored blue suit. There were women clamoring around him, some who obviously knew him and many who wanted to. As he turned around, his ringlets bounced and his first step was a confident one. That's when I realized I was staring at rapper-actor Ice-T.

Just then, I was tapped on the shoulder from behind by the guys I'd come with and was told it was time to leave. With one last look at Ice-T, I reluctantly followed behind the guys. There was something about Ice that kept me thinking about him for the rest of the night. He exuded confidence and power, and even without speaking to him, I could tell he had it all together and that being surrounded by all those women didn't excite him nearly as much as it excited them. He was used to it, and any one of those women would be better serviced by being with him, whereas he was already made and needed no woman to make him. I returned to Chuck's apartment that night, confident that I wanted to live in the City of Lost Angels.

On the set of Mystikal's "Danger" video shoot, Los Angeles.
(ARNOLD TURNER / NOOIMAGES-LA)

*I*n 2001, with DMX, on the set of Aaliyah's posthumous video shoot for "I Miss You," Los Angeles.

*W*ith Irv Gotti, at the 2002 *Lady of Soul Awards*, Los Angeles.

*G*reeting Ja Rule at the 2002 *Lady of Soul Awards.*

𝒲ith Al of MTV's *Punk'd*, at the Los Angeles airport.

𝒲ith Larenz Tate, on the set of the *A Man Apart*, Los Angeles.

𝒲ith F. Gary Gray at my twenty-sixth birthday party, in Los Angeles.

With Lil' Zane on the set of his video shoot for "None Tonight," Los Angeles.

With Bobby Brown on the set for his and Ja Rule's "Thug Lovin" video, Hollywood.

*I*n 2004, at a photo shoot for *XXL* magazine, Los Angeles.

EGO POP

*W*ith my son, Naiim, after my split with Kool G Rap.

(K. STEFFANS)

The next evening I put a call in to Marquis, and we talked for about an hour. Once he began to ask me about myself, I went on about all the things I had been through with G and how I had no idea what was to come back in Phoenix. All of a sudden, with a sense of urgency in his voice, he said, "There is someone you should meet. I think he could help you. Let me see if I can find him and call you back."

I waited nervously by the phone for about twenty minutes before it rang again. Marquis said hello and then checked to see if his friend was on the line, "Ice, you there?"

Another voice chimed in: "Yeah, I'm here."

Marquis continued: "Yizette, this is Ice-T. He's a good friend of mine, and I told him about you and your son and what you guys are going through right now. He can help you. Go ahead, Ice."

Ice spoke to me for a few minutes and gave me his number. He said he didn't want to say much over the phone and that we should meet the following day. The next day Chuck had returned from Hawaii to meet the moving trucks that would be taking him to a new house he had just purchased, and I was going to a hotel close to the airport since I would be leaving the following morning. Once I checked into the hotel, I immediately called Ice and asked him to meet me there. Within an hour, he was at the door.

I opened the door and let him in. It was sort of uncomfortable, meeting him for the first time. I was nervous and hopeful that he would say or do something that would change the course of my life. He sat on the end of the bed as I sat at the adjacent desk, telling him my story from start to finish, as my son crawled around, playing on the floor.

The look in his eyes softened more and more as I related the events of my life and relationship with G. I told him I was on my way back to Phoenix to tie up some loose ends and try to get an apartment and a job, but I'd decided to eventually move to Los Angeles. He told me his heart went out to me and my son and that he had been very affected by my story when Marquis had first told it to him, but was especially moved now, as he sat there watching my son and me together. He gave me some money, about three hundred dollars, and said that if I needed anything while in Phoenix, to be sure he was the first person I called. He also assured me that when I was ready to move to Los Angeles, he would see to it that I was taken care of until I was settled. I'd found a true friend and went back to Phoenix with a sense of security and a new strength. I had a way out and it was available to me whenever I was ready to take it.

Over the next ten months, I stayed in Phoenix. I was determined to put my failed marriage and everything that had occurred before it behind me. Since G and I had been separated, I had moved into my own apartment and worked several odd jobs trying to make ends meet, including a stint as a car salesperson. I settled on taking a quick nurse's-aid course and got placed in a nursing-assistant position at a senior-care hospital. Then, finally, I worked as an apartment-leasing consultant.

G, in the meantime, was in and out of town, living between New York and Arizona, as he worked to revitalize his career. He'd somewhat downgraded his lifestyle and no longer lived in the house we shared. Instead, he rented a three-bedroom apartment in a Phoenix suburb and lived with his girlfriend Ashley, who he'd moved from New York. He also began to spend large amounts of money on diamond and platinum jewelry, while I continued to struggle with our son.

G and I ended up living about four blocks apart, so he'd stop by my apartment to see me and the baby. Never once did I think of going back. I did, however, think we could at least work together to do the right thing for our son. I was wrong. Eventually, I saved enough money to buy my first car, a Nissan Sentra. I was so excited that I called G to tell him. His first words to me were, "Why would you buy a car? Take it back, and I'll buy you one later."

The summers in Phoenix were scorching, with temperatures upward of 120 degrees. Until I bought the car, I had been walking with my son to and from the grocery store while dodging four lanes of traffic. I had been wasting money on cabs, or waiting for G to give me a ride whenever he was in town.

In response to his telling me to take the car back, I simply told him I would and hung up the phone, knowing that G still didn't want the best for me or my son. I knew him well enough to know that he had no intention of buying me a car. He just wanted me to take the car back because he couldn't stand for me to be independent. Well, too late. I knew this car was the best thing for me, and I would no longer allow him to dictate my life.

I called Ice to tell him about the car, and he was happy for me. He was my support system, the only person in my life who was building me up, whereas everyone else seemed to be tearing me down. I began to no longer look for G's approval and counted on only Ice to be my guide. We would talk on the phone at least once a week. He sent money when I needed it and gave me advice, like only he could do. He told me there was no way I would make it in Phoenix and I needed to get to Los Angeles right away. He felt it was futile for him to continue sending me money in a place where I could never get ahead. Ice continually reassured me that I was meant to be something greater than I was. I was living in a one-bedroom apartment with no furniture, and the money I made with my job barely paid the accumulating bills and child-care expenses. Not to mention the enormous amount of debt I took on once G left me with all the bills from the house. I was ready to go, and Ice was behind me all the way.

It wasn't long before I filed papers at the local court-house for regulated child support and shared custody, but it would prove to be a slow-moving process. G pitched in financially once in a while, but it never seemed to be enough. I was in school and working part-time while G was living the high life, being the rap star he always wanted to be.

I wanted the chance to start over, too, in another city. It was my turn to get my life together. I was also angry because I had been doing all of the parenting by myself, and while G was getting his life in order, I felt confined by our child. I just needed a break, a chance to grow and learn and be someone different, someone other than this needy woman I had become. I wanted to be who I was before I met him—the confident, fearless, single me. There was just one thing I had to do before leaving Arizona . . . temporarily leave my son behind. Just in case I was making the wrong move, just in case I failed, I didn't want Naiim to fail with me. I wanted to be stable before bringing my son along, and although G and I had our problems, I knew he would never harm his son. While I'm not proud of the way I went about it, what I did next set me on the road to Los Angeles, without my son.

I drove the few blocks to G's apartment and arrived there just in time to see him getting into his car with a friend who was visiting from out of town. Impulsively, I sped up to the rear of G's car, and with a swift turn of the steering wheel, I blocked him in. My heart was pounding and all the sounds around me became muted. I flung open my car door, jumped out, and opened the back passenger door. I took my one-year-old son from his seat, grabbed his bag, and placed them both in the parking lot in front of G and his friend. And just as fast as I sped in, I hurried out before he could protest, and didn't stop until I hit the Hollywood city limits.

Each of those six hours felt like a hundred as I drove to Los Angeles. Ice had given me directions and reserved a suite for me at a hotel. I called him every hour to let him know the trip was going well. Along the way, I fantasized about what my new life would be like. I imagined the clothes and the cars. My mind traveled back to the women in the videos who I admired and I imagined myself looking just like them. I was happy, but more importantly, I was focused.

The journey ended at Franklin and Orchid Avenues in the heart of Hollywood. The street was dark and narrow, with a row of tiny hotels and tenements on each side. I took a deep breath before I entered the building. I was in shock. I pulled it off. I actually left it all behind: my old man, my old house, my old life, my new baby—my new baby.

I picked up the room key at the front desk. Once I was settled, there was a soft knock at the door and my heart seemed to skip a thousand beats. I straightened my clothes, smoothed out my hair, took another deep breath, and flung the door as wide as it would go until it hit the adjacent wall. I jumped into Ice-T's arms and held on as tight as I could. I smelled him, taking in every molecule.

Ice and I spent most every day together. I craved to be near him. I needed him. I needed Ice to teach me, to make me better, and to undo all of the awful things that had been done to me. Ice taught me a lot about how to make it in Los Angeles—where to eat, where to shop, how to negotiate, and to know my worth professionally. He also taught me about the Hollywood nightlife, and we'd frequent some of the hottest clubs in the city, yet he wasn't about dancing and partying. He observed. It was typical for us to grab a spot in the far right corner, always in position so Ice could see everyone who came and went and what they were doing. He usually wore a hat of some sort, sat with his legs crossed, appearing as if he was deep in thought. He rarely moved until it was time to go.

On the nights when we stayed in—and there were many—Ice and I would just quietly lie together, enjoying each other's presence. Sometimes, we drove around in his black-on-black S600 Mercedes, and I held his hand. Ice taught me that I should never hold someone's hand completely, just the smallest finger. This would show that I'm not asking for all of him, just a small part. And from that day forward, I would hold his pinkie finger and love that small part of him.

We spent a lot of time at his office in Hollywood, where he had a "pimp room." The office was on the top floor of the building and it overlooked the city. The pimp room had oversize red velvet curtains and black leather sofas. There were a few accessories that stood out—a giant "pimp-tionary," a dictionary of pimp terminology, and a video-camera set upon a tripod. In this room we watched porn and made a few flicks of our own. When we were together, I felt like a woman. I was all his.

I remember that first Christmas in Los Angeles. It fell on a Sunday, and he told his then longtime girlfriend and their young son that he was going to the bank or something. He came over and spent time with me so I wouldn't be alone. We both knew there was really no excuse for him not to be home on Christmas morning since everything was closed, but that never mattered to us. He operated in his own space and time. No one made Ice do anything he didn't want to do.

When we made love, it was never sexual; rather, it was like he was feeding me. With every slow, wet stroke, with every warm, sweet kiss, he gave me pieces of himself and let me know that he trusted and cared for me. I felt grown-up, knowing I could please a man like that—a man with so many more years and experiences than me. At those moments, I felt complete.

Chapter Nine

PAIN IS LOVE

ONCE I HAD BEEN IN HOLLYWOOD for a few weeks and had regained a certain amount of confidence, I was ready to try out my new life. It was January 2000, and I was twenty-one years old. I still felt unworthy of any kind of praise or acceptance, but all I needed was the right outfit and enough makeup to mask these insecurities. One afternoon I turned away from MTV for a moment to gather another pile of out-dated clothes, and just then, something drew me back to the TV screen. It was a new voice. It was raspy and commanding and the words were sharp and titillating. The singer's skin was dark and his body was cut. He seemed short, but still very big in presence. I waited intensely for the end of the song so I could read the credits and commit his name to memory. It read "JA Rule," and I whispered his name as if to place it onto my lips for tasting and followed that with "I want that one."

I drove to the Garden of Eden, a popular nightclub just three blocks from my hotel and one which Ice and I had gone to pretty frequently. I went alone that night, as would become typical for me. The club was very crowded, so I settled in at the bar. I felt I had better start drinking and fast because I was so nervous. Although I'd worked as a dancer in strip clubs, this was different. I had never been to a club before just to socialize and I wasn't sure what to do. I was certain that the liquor would tell me.

I mingled a bit, and before long, I grew increasingly bored. I was new to the club scene in this respect and hadn't found the purpose of it all. There was a whole upstairs portion to the club that I hadn't discovered where they housed the VIP section. After a few bats of the eyelashes and a smile or two, I was let up. It took about two minutes after I entered the VIP section before it happened—I saw him and had to blink twice. I was looking at him, and couldn't believe he was looking at me.

As I stared, he flooded his bloodshot eyes with eyedrops. Then he made his way toward me, and I swallowed so hard it felt like I popped an eardrum. I didn't hear or see anything else around me. His mouth opened, and in some sort of cinematic slow motion, he began to speak to me. I thought for sure I wouldn't be able to hear him, since everything else seemed to have faded to white noise, but his voice was clear. *Oh, God help me!* I thought. Ja Rule—the man I'd seen in the video for the first time earlier that night in my hotel room—was talking to me.

He was beautiful. The way those first few words sashayed beyond his lips and slammed into mine, the confidence he embodied. He was just as I thought he would be, the way he was on the television. It was like he heard my words and followed me here, just to make my wish of wanting to meet him come true.

We quickly got the formalities out of the way. "Hi, how are you?" he asked. "Where are you from?"

Blah. Blah. Blah. To tell the truth, all I wanted at that exact moment was for him to touch me, to take me with him. I felt inadequate, but I put on a confident front. *God, I hope he doesn't see through this lie,* I thought to myself. And just as I felt him moving closer to me, he abruptly turned to look behind him. Then he backed away, looking at me and shrugging his shoulders as if to say *Sorry.*

I knew she wasn't a girlfriend or wife. I could tell from her posture that she was just as insecure at the moment as me. As soon as I came to that conclusion, I became more determined than ever, as if her self-doubt fueled my assurance. *Let the games begin,* I thought. Just as this ran through my head, the lights came on and it was time to go. I would not let him get away from me. *He may be going home with her tonight. But starting tomorrow, he will be mine.*

I scrambled around, looking for a piece of paper, a napkin, anything to write on, and I pulled a nearly inkless pen from my purse. Just as he got a few paces past me, I trotted behind, grabbed his left hand (as she held his right), and pressed my name and number into his fist. He looked at me and smiled as I brushed past and walked ahead of them, through the doors. He was mine.

Ja Rule and I would talk over the next four months but were not able to see each other because he was busy with his career and I was busy still settling into my new life in L.A. Meanwhile, I decided to fly to New York on January 17, 2000, to pick up my son just days before his second birthday. G had taken him there, and although we had only been apart for one month, I just couldn't go on without my son any longer. Having my son in Los Angeles would make my transition harder, but not having him made everything else impossible.

I went straight from the airport to G's family's house in Queens. As is typical for a New York City winter night, it was bone-chilling cold, around seventeen degrees. An old friend of mine had picked me up at the airport and waited outside in the car as I got my son. This was not the same house in which I'd stayed with G and his mother prior to my son being born. This was the house where G's mother had died. Her spirit was still there; I could feel her.

However, G was nowhere to be found, as usual. He'd dropped Naiim off with a cousin the moment he arrived in New York from Phoenix. When I arrived, I was distraught to find that my son, at just two years old, was drinking sugary grape Kool-Aid and had a newly acquired rotten front tooth. G's whole family had bad teeth and now I could see why. G's teeth would fall out and chip every time he ate, and his brother, at forty, had no teeth at all. This was definitely nowhere for my son to be, and regardless of the hardships ahead, I knew Naiim would be better off with me. I hastily grabbed him and his suitcase and jetted out the house, using my waiting friend as an excuse for my rush. Happy to be with my son again, we flew back to Los Angeles, and I was ready for whatever awaited us.

Having my son with me in Los Angeles allowed me to feel more complete. But unfortunately, it didn't stop me from continuing to enjoy the nightlife. I hired a sitter and began going out as much as I possibly could. The next few months went by pretty fast. Although Ja Rule and I continued to grow close with our frequent phone conversations, I found myself juggling a few new people in my life as well.

While I waited for Ja to head back to Los Angeles, I became friendly with Fred Durst, the lead singer of Limp Bizkit. We met on a clear, winter day. The sun was bright, and although the breezes were chilly, the overall temperature was unseasonably warm. I was pulling into the underground parking garage of Interscope Records in Westwood. As I pulled in, he was pulling out. Our eyes met, and I recognized the face but couldn't place it. After hesitating a bit, I kept going. All of a sudden his SUV stopped. He blared his horn and reversed his car with force.

We casually introduced ourselves and he blurted, "Don't you know who I am?"

I responded, "Um . . . no, should I?" I already loved his cockiness.

"I'm Fred Durst . . . from Limp Bizkit! I'm the senior vice president of this company! Who are you going up there to see?"

I was caught for a moment in the sea that was his eyes. Crystal blue, piercing through me and making me want him. I could smell the power oozing from his pores, and I was so turned on, I knew I'd need a shower after this encounter.

"I'm going to see my boy, Big Chuck," I sputtered as he cut me off to tell me that he knew Chuck really well and that he thought I was beautiful. As he hopped down from his SUV, his physical appearance delighted me. This big man was actually kind of small. He had this swagger about him that commanded attention. We exchanged numbers and I listened intently to every word he said as I watched his lips beckon to me. He said he would be back at the office in a few hours and he would call me then. I remained outwardly calm, but inside I was overwhelmed. I was mesmerized and flattered. Once he sped off, I was alone with my drifting thoughts.

Breathing once again, I actually jumped around a bit, which is embarrassing to admit. I regained my composure and headed up to see Chuck. My time at the Interscope offices was brief, but I hesitated to leave. Like a girl with a high school crush, I thought, *What if Fred calls and I can't get to him in time? What if I never see him again?* So as the parking garage emptied, I stayed and waited for Fred to call me. Finally, we spoke, but I was too ashamed to mention that I was still outside the garage where we had met three hours prior. I went back to my hotel room exhausted from hoping and pretending, but I was also determined he would not get away from me.

By April 2000, Ja Rule and I had spoken so much over the phone since the first night we met that I had grown to know him pretty well. He was coming back to Los Angeles after spending a few weeks on the East Coast. I couldn't wait.

L'Ermitage, an über-luxury hotel on Burton Way in the heart of Beverly Hills. Room 416. When I think back to this night, it's funny to recall how, in the midst of such grandeur, I was so casually attired. I was in my then-typical casual wear of jeans and T-shirt, with my hair pulled back into a modest ponytail. Yet I was seduced by the luxury and posh detail that surrounded me at L'Ermitage. I arrived at the room and knocked lightly on the door before I realized that it was already ajar. I slowly opened it farther and stuck my head in. "Hello?" The lights were dim and the radio was tuned to 92.3 FM. The songs were slow favorites and I began to hum along as I walked in, feeling comfortable. I put down the overnight bag I had packed in anticipation. I looked around a bit but was really afraid to move too much for fear of disturbing the ambience. I sucked it all in. I could taste it. Just then, he walked in. He was short and dark, just like the drink he held, lazily swirling it around in a glass. As he stood there staring at me, all he wore was a white hotel bathrobe and bed slippers. I just wanted to run to him and tear him apart. I wanted to suck his mouth and taste the liquor, to lick his neck and chest. I wanted the salt of his sweat to help me chase the heat of his kiss.

Before I finished that thought, I had him there in my mouth, and in those moments I was a beast. He squirmed and twisted his body in ways that almost frightened me. It seemed as if he would snap in two or even spontaneously combust from the pressure of screaming into a down-filled pillow. I had him, I knew it. What I was doing to his body was new to him and especially new to me. As I sucked and licked, he screamed, and suddenly grabbed both of his ankles as he threw them into the air. I was powerful at this moment. I'd discovered something new—I had the power here.

Glass vases filled with marbles crashed all around us as he began tossing linens from the bed. As the marbles scattered, we laughed in unison. We were just beginning. The rest of the night we explored countless positions. I remember the exact moment that I first lay on my back for him. I looked up at him as he knelt before me. My legs were wrapped around his waist, and just before his body was to merge with mine, I noticed his upper right chest. On it was a tattoo with the words PAIN IS LOVE. I ran my fingers over the prophetic words. Ja entered my body and I felt both pain and love, simultaneously. As I looked to the ceiling above, I cried silently and the words of the Isley Brothers' "Voyage to Atlantis" played in my head.

As the first warm tear rolled into my ear, I whispered to him, "Promise you'll always come back to me . . . promise you'll always come back to me . . . please." With his cheek against my tear-soaked face, he promised me. I believed him.

Ja and I went at each other in this fashion over the next five days. The phone rang and there were knocks at the door, but he didn't seem to care. Neither did I. He made it okay for us to disappear into our own lust-filled world. He was in the same place as I was—pure bliss. I was a virgin before him in so many ways, and on that night, the cherry was popped on the rest of my life. To me, he was my first real lover since G, and I ate him alive. That first night turned into five days, and by the time the rest of Murder Inc. was allowed in the room, we were both in heaven. We began to sing each other's praises, like jocks in a locker room, as I began to recite a verse from Jadakiss, *"Got a chick named Super-head / She give super head / Just moved in the buildin, even gave the super head . . ."* We all laughed, and then between us, the name stuck. It was an insider's joke that was supposed to forever remind us of the first time Ja and I connected. It, and I, belonged to Murder Inc. However, the rest of the close-knit hip hop industry would soon catch wind of our little joke, and it would quickly turn into something not so funny. What had started out as an incredibly personal pet name eventually and quickly turned into my scarlet letter. It would be taken out of context from that day forward.

On our last day, Ja left the room before I woke up. I felt energized and was ready to see the world again. I looked around for something to take with me, something that would smell like him but wouldn't be missed. On the floor I found a balled-up sock, and I placed it to my face and got the fix I was searching for. I could smell his skin and the aroma of the hotel room, and that would be enough to hold me until I could see my love again.

Ice and I hadn't seen each other much, and the only time we really spoke was when I ran out of money. He supported my spending habits and helped me take care of my son's needs. Ice never demanded any of my time. He understood me and knew I had to go out and find my own way. With the lessons he taught me, like where to go to meet influential people and how to dress and speak, he always knew I would be okay. It's why my love for him is genuine and complete.

So with a decent amount of money at my disposal, I was able to pay someone to take care of my son around the clock while I shopped and gradually became the quintessential urban socialite, albeit one with access to hip hop royalty.

Fred Durst and I continued to stay in touch and soon we had our official first date. We met at PF Chang's at the Beverly Center Mall for lunch, and even though we had spoken quite a bit, I was still extremely nervous around him. I remember feeling like I had to try extra hard to impress him, as if I just wasn't good enough. He was different from the others. He wasn't flashy and flamboyant. He was more laidback and introverted. I never knew what he was thinking and wanted to be sure he had no reason to not like me.

We sat and talked and got to know each other more, but something happened at the table that stayed with me. Fred ordered five different entrées, just for himself. I was confused but didn't want to seem young and inexperienced, so I just watched his movements. He seemed to be the same as me, a bit depressed and lonely, a stranger to love, and searching. He opened up to me about himself, and I felt special. Just as his story was getting good, our food was served—my one plate and his five. For the next forty-five minutes, while we sat there in the booth and discovered each other, I watched him move. He was grand, taking tiny forkfuls from each dish and repeating that move a few times. Then, just that fast, he was done, leaving the majority of the food behind. I was in awe. I had never really wasted food before, and right then I knew that one day I would be able to eat whatever I wanted, however much I wanted, and summon someone to take the plates away. In my inexperienced mind, it was the height of glamour. With all of his tattoos, body piercing, and worn way of dress, Fred had an air of prestige to me. I silently hoped for him to want me.

After we ate, I accompanied him to the studio to watch him record. He let me read his lyric book. He'd written the most hateful words about love and the lack thereof. There were pictures he had drawn of people he knew and images which were unrecognizable and disturbing at the same time. Still, I only wanted him more. I wanted to love him, to heal him. I felt he might want the same and perhaps that's why he was sharing so much of himself with me.

He took several pictures of me with his digital camera. It was the first time I had seen one. He took close-up pictures of my breasts, which he wanted to put onto his computer for him to admire at his leisure. Crazy as it sounds now, I thought the idea was sexy at the time. That night I begged him to take me with him, but he resisted. Instead, he walked me to my car, where I found a forty-dollar parking ticket, which I ripped to pieces before settling into my car for the lonely drive home. But before I made it to the driver's seat, I turned around right into a kiss—his kiss. Those few moments were like hours to me. His lips were soft and surprisingly full as I sucked his kiss.

"Please don't make me go," I begged. "Please . . ."

Fred looked right through me with those eyes of his and said, "I have to."

I opened my car door slowly, hoping he would change his mind within the eight seconds it would take me to sink into my seat. As he looked on, that's exactly what I did, I sank into my seat, closed the door, and, through my tears, found my way back to the hotel.

Early spring was also when I met one of the most significant members of the hip hop community. He is so different from the rest, I refuse to name him. For the sake of identity, I'll call him Papa. I remember seeing Papa on television when I was a thirteen-year-old girl, when I first discovered him. Videos were new to me, and although I wasn't familiar with hip hop, I was becoming familiar with him. I would race home from school just to catch *Rap City* on BET and hoped they hadn't shown his video yet. Eventually, I got wise and started taping the episodes. I would freeze-frame his face and stare at it, wishing I was older and out there in the world so I could bump into him somewhere, somehow. Fast-forward eight years and there he was, standing right in front of me.

I met Chuck on the set of yet another video shoot, to hang out. Still new to the scene, I felt self-conscious. I wasn't like the other girls on the set. Despite my trysts with Ice-T and Ja Rule, I felt plain and unworthy. After years of hearing how worthless I was from my mother and then G, my self-confidence was wavering at best. As I looked around the set, trying to settle my nerves, I noticed him. I wanted to go over and say hello, to be as brash as I had been with Ja, but I couldn't move. Just as I was about to give up on the notion, Chuck called me over. I looked in Papa's direction and stopped breathing. I walked over, slowly, only looking at Chuck, as if I hadn't noticed Papa standing there, as if I hadn't been seducing him with my eyes the entire night.

As I was talking to Chuck, pretending to ignore Papa, he grabbed my phone out of my hand and walked away with it.

"Let me use this for a minute," he said.

I thought it was strange, his needing my phone, but I was content just to have had some sort of contact with him. I continued talking to Chuck, and a few seconds later Papa returned and placed the phone back in my hands. For some reason, without looking, I started clearing the screen.

"You're not clearing your screen, are you?" Papa said.

"Yeah, why?" I answered nervously. I couldn't believe we were actually having an exchange.

"Look at it," he said.

I looked at the phone and felt like a child. How could I not have realized what he'd done? It was his phone number.

"What was that last number again?" I smirked.

"Two."

In person, Papa was just as I had imagined him to be eight years before as I watched his videos. He was funny and charming, and his eyelashes curled perfectly above his almost squinty eyes. He had so much charisma and confidence. He was sure of himself and well respected among other men. I loved him instantly. Love, in a sense, had always been easy for me. I loved the idea of it and have loved many men in my life. But only one man would be the recipient of my ongoing devotion, no matter what. And that's why, although it felt awkward and artificial to call Kool G Rap "Daddy," it was more than fitting to call the man who would steal my heart over and over again "Papa."

PAIN
IS
LOVE

Chapter Ten

AROUND THE BLOCK

IN APRIL 2000, Ice had set me up in a two-bedroom condo in Santa Clarita, about thirty minutes north of Beverly Hills. A few weeks later, he landed a great-paying gig on *Law & Order: Special Victims Unit* and was headed to New York. Ice had been my safety net, and I knew that if I got myself into any trouble, he would help me out. But now he had some bad news.

"Hey, babe," he said. "I have to let you go."

He said he was pretty sure that with the skills he had given me, I would be okay.

"You'll be more than okay," he said. "You're going to make it. And when you do, find me and buy me a white Benz." I've held on to those words all of these years. I made the promise, and I meant it.

"Bye, Ice."

"Good-bye, baby girl."

Meanwhile, Fred and I hadn't spoken much after our date, but Chuck insisted that Fred was really into me. So I naively continued to play cat and mouse with him, via his voice mail. Once in a while, he would call me back. I wanted him more than ever, but he was elusive. I found myself fantasizing about him day and night. I made up things in my head, and whenever I did speak to him, I took all of his words to heart and sometimes even out of context. I wanted to believe that all those sparks I felt when we were together were real, that I didn't imagine them.

Then, finally, we got together. My hands shook as I drove to his office, speeding along the 405 freeway. I checked my makeup and popped a few mints. My breathing was heavy and so were my expectations. Walking down the long hallway to his opened door, I whispered to myself "Relax," and "Breathe." The office was officially closed, so most everyone in the building was gone for the day, with the exception of a few stragglers. As I approached Fred's doorway, I felt a quivering in my knees and thought I would just drop to the floor.

His voice saved me. "Close the door," he said.

His workspace looked mostly like a living room, so I kicked off my shoes and joined him on one of the sofas. We talked for a while, but I really don't remember much of the conversation because as his lips were moving, all I wanted to do was inch closer to them. I didn't want to talk; we had done enough talking. I wanted my turn on this ride. So, while he was in midsentence, I interrupted by gently biting then pulling his bottom lip. He grabbed the back of my head and fused our mouths together. I grabbed on to his flesh and heaved myself across his lap, straddling this wild man. Before I could begin to own this intensity, I was on my knees. I looked at his pierced penis with a sick admiration. He was what I wanted, and to actually hold him in my hand at that time felt like a privilege. He was allowing me to finally have him, to taste him. And again, I felt powerful here.

I was turned on by the fact that this was a man who so many women wanted, and this man wanted me. Onstage, he commanded crowds of people, millions, and at this very moment I commanded him. It was as if he and I had traded places in the world, and I was important. At that moment, and moments like it, I didn't feel inadequate or mediocre.

"Make me cum and I'll marry you," were the only words I remember Fred saying to me.

I was so caught up that for a hot minute I might even have believed him. But before I knew it, my power trip was over. Few words were spoken and I was basically dismissed. Leaving was awkward and plain awful. Reality set in: I'd allowed myself to be seduced by the dream and the wake-up call was harsh and unpleasant. I left Fred's office feeling dejected, and even more than that, naive and silly.

After my encounter with Fred Durst, I was in need of a self-esteem boost. I looked up Ja Rule, and we continued to hang out throughout the summer. Our nights consisted of plenty of sex, drugs, and liquor. We walked around the hotel in our robes. His suite always seemed to be full of people— label executives, other artists, women, hangers-on, you name it. We drank heavily and popped XTC pills in rapid succession. We traveled in huge numbers and bounced from club to club. I felt I was a part of something real for the first time in my life. I was liked and accepted, and the perks were addicting. We could go anywhere and do anything. Everyone watched when we moved and all the other girls wanted to come along. I was where other people wanted to be and felt special.

There are quite a few memories of my time with Ja that will always stay with me. We used to have deep conversations about anything and everything. We spoke about his personal struggles and career plans. He spoke tenderly of his family, his grandmother, and a sister who'd died sometime before. In tribute to her, he has a tattoo of her name and angel wings on his back.

In the midst of my trysts with Ja Rule, I still longed to be involved with Papa, but he was ignoring me. For four straight months, I called, with no response. Yet I refused to give up. I needed the acknowledgment. Then he finally called me. When I heard his voice on the other end of the phone, my eyes began to tear. I was exasperated but remained composed. The meeting was set, and I was on my way.

As I was getting closer to the studio to meet Papa, I began to notice that familiar feeling of insecurity. My hair wasn't right, my clothes weren't new, and I just wasn't up to par. But when I arrived at the studio and began to take the long, winding walk to the back room, all eyes were on me. My self-doubt disappeared with each step. When he saw me again for the first time in four months, his eyes seemed to dance. He instantly grabbed his backpack and we left.

We talked all the way to his hotel. He made me laugh and then, to my surprise, I made him laugh, too. He was really listening to me and liked what I had to say! It was as if we'd known each other for years and we were friends. I didn't feel nervous or inadequate. I felt beautiful and appreciated. I was dizzy with delight and for a moment the reality whizzed through my head: I was with *him*. I had admired him from afar as a young girl and dreamed of this moment almost a decade before, and here he was, and he was interested in me! As we walked into the Beverly Hills Hotel bungalow, an overwhelming need to prove my worthiness came over me. It was as if I had to show him I was worth keeping around, that I was worthy of his presence. I had to thank him for choosing me and do it in a fashion that would make him want to keep choosing me for years to come. Once again, I turned to sex.

He sat in a chair in the living room and turned on the television. I'm pretty sure that there was some sort of verbal exchange, but I blocked it out. The only thing I registered was the insatiable need to feast, to take from him. I needed to feel his energy and rock him to the core. Without thinking, I dropped to my knees before him and began to tear away at his clothes. His reaction was surprising, as if he didn't expect this. But after he found his home in the warm, wet confines of my mouth and throat, he lay back and exhaled.

My body was on fire, and as I worked on Papa, I began ripping away at my clothes. I was at home here with him. I loved his body and this part of him that I wanted to ingest. He moved around in that chair to the point that it lifted off its front feet. There was a sort of levitation happening as we moved to the bedroom. I couldn't stop; I couldn't let our skin separate. It was as if he became my lifeline, my sexual IV. For the next six hours, he filled me up and then drained me. He pounded and he stroked, and he made me want to live and die at the same time. I thought my heart would stop and that I would take my last breath there on that bed. We were wet and sticking to each other, and with every breath he let go, I sucked in. He pulled me and pushed me and threw my body around, having his way. And from that day on, he would be my Papa.

Yet just like that, he, too, was gone. He just got up and walked out. It was six in the morning and he had a flight to catch. His home was a long way from Los Angeles, but I knew he'd be taking a part of me with him, which made me feel satisfied for the moment. I twirled around that hotel room like a schoolgirl with a new dress. I was walking on air. I was ready. I just wasn't sure for what.

Although I was hanging out with hip hop's elite and enjoying the best restaurants, had access to any club or party, and wore the hottest fashions, I had nothing to call my own or to support me and my son. When Ice-T left for New York, my sense of stability quickly faded. There was no safety net, so in many respects, I was back at square one. Not to mention, my drinking and experimentation with drugs had begun to get out of control, and I hadn't spent much time at all with my son. I became a hustler of sorts— bouncing in and out of strip clubs and selling myself in every way. I had gotten to a very desperate point where I could only have sex if it was accompanied by perks. I expected and received money from every man in my life, especially celebrities. I used sex to keep them happy, and when they were happy, they were generous. I needed to survive now that Ice was gone and I didn't know any other way. Plus, I'll be honest. I was good at using sex to get what I wanted and needed. That's all I knew.

In addition to using sex and depending on it to get what I wanted, I couldn't be alone. So I would pack clothes for a week or two and just bounce around. The condo had nothing in it really, because it wasn't a home. And I had no idea what it took to turn it into one. Ice taught me a lot of things about Los Angeles and survival. But no one ever taught me how to live.

I did experience genuine happiness around this time. I became involved with a young man. I was twenty-one, emotionally going on thirty-five, and he had just turned eighteen but physically looked much younger. I had seen him at a party the day before we met. We noticed each other, and those three seconds became six as we moved in slow motion around each other. Just as quickly, I blinked and he was gone. The following night, after another party, a girlfriend said she knew him and would take me to his house. Although he'd just turned eighteen, he already had his own home and vehicle and lived very much the life of an adult. We were let in by his cousin, who said Ray was sleeping upstairs. Soon Ray stumbled down the stairs, having just been woken up and coming off a late night out. His eyes opened wide and were immediately drawn to me. Almost like there were clouds under his feet, he floated toward me and we were introduced. "Hi, I'm Ray." You know him as Ray J, the younger brother of singer Brandy.

Not much else about that night was committed to my memory, but it began one of the happiest times in my life. It was easy to fall in love with Ray. He brought back a part of my youth that had been stolen from me years before. Ray was single, with no children, which equaled no drama. And at that time I lived my life the same way. So much so that I never told Ray about my son—or anything else about me for that matter. When I went out with him, I felt "official." I was a girlfriend, and that's entirely different from being just a lover.

Ray and I spent months together as I juggled him and Papa like a circus act. My relationship with Ray made Papa uncomfortable and even furious. Papa knew everything about me and accepted me just the way I was, but the one thing he could never tolerate was me *loving* someone else. And I loved Ray J. It was the first time since Papa and I met that I had given so much attention to another man. It was not normal, and Papa didn't appreciate the change. Now, when Papa needed me, I wasn't always available.

This new relationship was special to me because with Ray J, I had someone to spend time with in public, as a couple. We held hands and let people know we were together. I was proud of that. Because Ray is a member of a tight-knit, well-known family, it's not surprising that they didn't approve of me. They knew I was older than him and they were concerned for him. What's more, before meeting me, Ray had just gotten out of a longtime relationship with one of the members of the girl group 702. His family had become accustomed to her being part of his life, and here I was—a virtual stranger. Eventually, however, certain members of his family accepted us and we were free to enjoy our relationship.

When Ray and I made love, we would go for hours on end, each hour more satisfying than the last. Being with Ray was always sweet and innocent. His kisses were long and his lips were full and light as they met mine. He was young and still a bit inexperienced, and shied away from oral sex, but he would kiss all around my lower regions and make my body quiver just the same. It was with Ray that I discovered my ability to orgasm without penetration or copulation. I would be excited just from his touch. Ray was with me because he liked me. It was pure and this purity was so new to me that it had become more erotic than being with any other lover. After our lovemaking, we would pass out, him holding me and me feeling loved.

Ray and I created a stir around town and people began to wonder what it was I saw in him. He was so young and wasn't yet respected as a major player among men. What no one could've possibly realized was that it took a younger man to make me feel young again. We were silly together, and we enjoyed spending long afternoons and nights together. We saw our favorite movies, like *Big Momma's House*, starring Martin Lawrence and Nia Long, three or four times and enjoyed them each time as if it were the first time. I felt free with Ray. He awakened a desire in me to get my youth back and hold on tight.

Ice had come and gone, and Fred was out of the picture. But my relationship with Ja was ongoing and became more intense as we ate, drank, and slept together. Our sex became a constant in my life and he himself became the drug. I was also hooked on the atmosphere. Being around Ja Rule and Murder Inc. felt like being around family, the one feeling I had always longed for. We all knew we were up to no good and I loved it—that is, until I found out that not only was Ja still in a relationship with his teenage sweetheart, but they were also expecting their second child.

I entered my relationships with Ice, Ja, and Papa knowing they had other women, though none was married. I remember the first time it really registered for me that Ja had another relationship and responsibilities, separate and apart from the carefree, wild life he led in Los Angeles. It was early one morning at the hotel, and whoever the other girl was we'd brought back with us the night before was gone—it was not uncommon for Ja and me to pick up other women and have threesomes. We were wild and disregarded all the conventional rules and authority. The phone rang, and I stayed quiet as Ja answered. The woman on the other end of the phone was frantic, not letting him get so much as a word in.

All he could squeeze in was, "What girl? Somebody told you what?"

He eventually slammed the phone down while the woman was still in midrant. He pulled me close as I lay on his chest and we passed out.

That's how it was with Ja. One crazy adventure after the next, and I was so out of it then that there are a lot of things I've long since forgotten. But then there are some incidents that I will never forget. Like the night I thought Ja was going to die. We were getting ready to go out, as usual, and true to form, we started popping XTC pills and guzzling Rémy Martin straight from the bottle. It seems as if he took more than usual from the time we woke up until about ten at night. This was a little scary.

He had disappeared for a while to another room—probably to be with other girls, which was also common. About forty-five minutes later, there was a soft, weak knock at the door. I opened it and there he stood in a cold sweat. He was shaking and having a hard time walking. There were a few other girls in the room with us and they all just stood there, watching. They were new to our clique. They didn't know Ja like I knew him. I led him into the bathroom, but before he could make it, he began to throw up.

At the time I was so caught up with Ja that all I was thinking was that I needed to protect him. I didn't want any vomit to touch his skin. I cared deeply for this man, regardless of anything or anyone else. Ja purged for a few minutes, and just like that, he was better. I offered to get him some water, but he refused. Instead, he grabbed the Rémy bottle, guzzled, and we kept the party going. Sadly, he was amazing that way. He never stopped. He was always "on" when others were around.

Meanwhile, Papa and I stayed in touch constantly. He had been working in Los Angeles a lot and I jumped at the chance to see him. He became my refuge at times. Unlike with Ja and Murder Inc., there were no wild parties, no entourages, no other girls, and no self-abuse. Our time together was quiet and special. We watched movies and ordered room service. He would preview his projects and let me hear his work. My favorite memories are of him giving me private live shows in his boxers. Most of all, we were friends—friends who also had incredible sex.

I accepted early on that no man is perfect. Although Papa was being unfaithful, he loved and valued his family and fiercely protected them from his life as an entertainer. I respected Papa's space and his privacy, and do so even now. It gave me chills when he spoke to his family in front of me. I felt privileged to be with him, a man who was so loved by the people in his life. He brought me a certain sense of calm. But it was typical of me to further complicate things, so it should be no surprise that somehow Dr. Dre entered the mix.

Chuck introduced Dre to me a week after I arrived in Los Angeles. Nothing happened right away, but when I visited Chuck on the set of one of Dre's videos, things quickly took a familiar turn. I met Dre at the Universal City Hilton near Universal Studios on June 8, 2000. Far from the luxury of L'Ermitage in Beverly Hills, Dre and I met in the hotel's Lobby Lounge, where we ordered drinks and made small talk. It was uneasy and awkward. We both knew what we were there to do, and I couldn't figure out why we were stumbling around it. I didn't find him terribly attractive physically or even sexually, and our personalities didn't particularly mesh. But power is an overwhelming thing. I felt important sitting there with him. Everyone knew his face, and I'm sure they suspected he was up to no good, being at the Hilton around midnight with a woman. But here in Hollywood, it's common and often expected.

Room 2257 was small and quaint, but it didn't matter. I

knew he wouldn't be staying long, so I cut the conversation short and joined him under the sheets. It was still very awkward, and it wasn't as if he drove me mad like Ja or Papa or even Fred. I felt nothing. I just knew this was an important man, one of the highest-paid, biggest-selling artist-producers in the world. As he got on top of me, I was empty and cold. I stared at his face, his eyes, and it was only when I ran his résumé and status through my head that my insides began to feel warmer. He left shortly afterward, and I was okay with that. Thinking back on it, I really don't know what led me to that hotel room and into Dre's bed. It was another example of my doing without thinking, for all the wrong reasons.

I hopped back on the merry-go-round and ran back to Ray, back to that place where I was safe and where having sex felt natural. Around this time, Ray had begun to work on an album. I remember vividly the night he recorded the song that would change everything. "Where Do We Go from Here" was a song about meeting someone and spending so much time with them, even beginning to love them, and wanting to know if it could, or should, be more. Ray stood in the recording booth, belted out that song, and accompanied it with tears. He cried, and I cried witnessing it.

I loved this boy so much and wanted nothing more than to stay with him. But I knew that one day I would have to go, that one day he would know who I had been with and render me unworthy of the affection he was now showing me. As much as I loved Ray, I was too deep in my lifestyle, with an undeniable reputation, to go back. I was still greedy. I wanted it all. I wanted Ray's love. I wanted the carefree, bling-filled lifestyle of hanging with the likes of Ja and the laid-back, mind-blowing sex and friendship I relished with Papa. And more than anything, I wasn't ready to settle down. The first time I'd tried to settle down with a man led to my wanting to die. I wasn't going back there. So I knew the end for Ray and me was near and inevitable.

Later that night, when the recording of the song was finished, we lay in bed and played it over and over. We held on to each other and cried silently. It was all so overwhelming, and I knew that night he loved me, too. Before long, it was time for him to go away and record in Atlanta. I knew the separation would be difficult, but I really thought we could make it. What I didn't know was that by this time, Ray was beginning to find out about me, and we were growing apart. I deeply wished I were someone different— that I was a normal girl without all the baggage, the sordid past. But I was who I was, and I had done what I had done. It was impossible to turn back. I couldn't undo all of the abuse and the men. If he wanted to leave, I couldn't stop him. Hell, I couldn't blame him.

What I could do, what I was also very good at, was run. And that's what I did. I ran right to Papa again. I ran to the man who accepted me and away from the boy I knew couldn't afford to. He was still in an impressionable stage of his life, and just the way I had swept in and made him think I was wonderful, his friends and peers in the industry would soon prove to him that the image I portrayed was all an illusion.

I almost wanted Ray to hate me so we could end it right there, quickly. In order to protect my heart, I wanted to let him go first because I knew he was about to do the same to me. So that's what I did. Late on a Saturday night, I called Ray and told him all about me and Papa. Naturally, he wasn't happy. He said some awful things to me, called me horrible names, and slammed down the phone. What he couldn't have known is that for the next six months, I cried every day for him. I genuinely missed him more than I'd missed any other man I'd ever known. When he hung up that night, it closed the door on a relationship that I still treasure.

However, this thing with me and Ja wouldn't stop. We spent a lot of time together, and as the months passed, he gained more and more notoriety as an artist and as a Hollywood bachelor. There were girls everywhere, and my position in his life became blurred. I was beginning to feel as if my time with him would be up soon. How right I was.

I was at Chuck's office one day just shooting the breeze when I picked up a copy of a music magazine. There was an article celebrating hip hop dads and their kids. This must have been around Father's Day. The magazine featured five or six fathers, including Ja. I knew he had a daughter who was about five at the time, but the article went on about him and his longtime girlfriend and how she was expecting another child. Although it was known that Ja had been with his teenage sweetheart for years, I found out in that article that while Ja and I had been together in Los Angeles, she was at home in New York pregnant.

The Ja I knew and the life he led . . . I chuckled to think of him as this family man. I thought to myself, *She's so stu-*

pid! I felt as if I was the one who knew everything; I was the gatekeeper of the treacherous secrets of his life while he was in Los Angeles. I finished the article with a smile on my face, until the last line. Ja's wife was five-months pregnant. It was the exact amount of time that I had been in his life. My heart sank, and I couldn't blink as my eyes swelled with tears. Who was stupid now? Who was getting the real Ja? Not me and not any of the other women who'd been part of his world. We were all replaceable and temporary; she, however, was permanent.

Later that night, I met up with him at a local club. All of his friends and label mates were there, so I tried for a long time to hide my pain. I laughed and ordered drinks, danced around and popped pills. I tried to appear normal, but inside, everything was different. He mingled and flirted relentlessly with other women. I felt the heat of jealousy crawling up my neck, blanketing my face. Then I blinked, took in a long slow breath, and snapped. I grabbed champagne bottles and glasses, whatever I could find, and hurled them at his head. I ranted and raved, cried and blurted out words that were sure to make him leave me right then and there.

He seemed confused as he called out to me, "Come here! Come here, crazy girl!"

I was afraid to move closer. There was a pool table between us, and that table may very well have saved my life. But even in the middle of all my chaos and acting out, he wouldn't let any of the others restrain me. It was like we had an unspoken understanding. He knew I was hurt and that my outburst could be justified. He might not have known exactly what caused it, but he knew that there were enough possibilities to choose from. He knew it was time, that it was the end.

I left the club shortly after and drove recklessly, crying uncontrollably. Like with any breakup, even if it is the right thing to do, I started to have regrets about my temper tantrum. I wasn't sure I was ready for it to be over despite the reality check. I didn't want to drive all the way home to my empty condo. Instead, I wanted him to tell me he understood why I had snapped and that I could be with him for the night. I wanted him to touch me like he had before, like he did on that first night.

So instead of going home, I drove to that familiar street where my life in L.A. had all started. I drove to Orchid Avenue, parked in front of the Orchid Suites Hotel, and dialed his number. He sounded tired and uninterested in what I had to say, but didn't hang up.

"Ja, I'm sorry. It was the drinks and then I took some X, and I just got all emotional. Baby, I'm so sorry . . ."

I cried out to him to forgive me. I wanted for him to feel sorry for me and to let me come to him.

"It's cool, Ma. Don't worry about it." The tone of his voice said it all. He was done with me.

I sat in my car that night and cried until it hurt. My eyes, my throat, my chest—it all hurt. I sat there in my car, thinking about the hotel in front of me, wondering how I'd gotten into this mess. I wanted my old room back. I wanted to be back sitting among those outdated clothes. I wanted to undo the moment when I stepped into my first club, the moment when I popped my first pill. I wished I had never seen Ja's face—or any of their faces. I wanted so badly to be a little girl minus the rape, the mother-daughter drama, and the men. The only beacon of light was my son and my relationship with Papa. He was all I had left. Back then, I just couldn't stand the idea of being alone.

AROUND
THE
BLOCK

Chapter Eleven

VIDEO GIRL

BY THIS TIME, I had known most of the employees at Def Jam Records and had visited their offices on Sunset Boulevard, which were perched on the top floor of the Hustler Building. A girlfriend of mine and I had gone to an LL Cool J video shoot in order to meet with one of Def Jam's employees.

Within seconds, my eyes landed on the person we were there to meet. We sat and talked for a few moments before another man came over and introduced himself to me.

"Hey, I'm Hype," he said casually. "What are you doing next week?"

I was taken aback and wasn't quite sure who he was, yet I answered, "Nothing."

He continued, "Okay, cool. Take my number and call me. You're going to be in my next video. Get a tan."

Then I realized that this was famed music-video director Hype Williams. It would be my first video, and the following weekend I was on the set of Jay-Z's video for his single "Hey Papi."

Days before arriving on the set, I called Chuck to let him know that I would be working on the video. Chuck and Jay had been good friends for years, and I wanted Jay to know that I was coming. By this time, Chuck and I were closer than ever and continued to claim each other as cousins, though we weren't blood relatives. So Chuck made the call to be sure that once on-set, I would be taken care of. Call time was early, around six in the morning. We were on location at Zuma Beach in Malibu, and all the talent had convened in the hair and makeup trailers to begin the long preparation process. I was a bundle of nerves but tried my best to remain cool among the other girls. My heart raced, and I was excited to get up to the house where we would be working. I was anxious to meet Jay and introduce myself to him since I was also a fan of his music. Finally, the moment arrived.

We were shuttled up a winding hill to a palatial mansion overlooking Zuma. This was my first time in a house this size and in Malibu. This was also the first time Jay and I would speak. As soon as we unloaded from the van, I saw Jay standing poolside in front of Hype and his camera. I quickly made my way over to introduce myself.

"Hey, I'm Yizette," I said, "Chuck's people."

"Yeah?" he said. "What's up? Chuck told me you was

coming. Come on. You stand by me all day today." And that was it.

For the rest of the day, I stood as close as possible to Jay. I became acquainted with his entourage, as well as with his partner, Damon Dash. The performer in me was evident throughout the day as I did the most outrageous things possible, like wearing an ultraskimpy string thong bikini, while the other girls proudly sported modest full-back bikinis and one-piece bathing suits.

The atmosphere became tense between me and the other girls almost instantly. The majority of girls on video shoots are reserved and are there strictly to do their jobs. As a silent rule, the feature girls never fraternized with the artists and, in many cases, actually looked down their noses at the artists. They walked with their heads high, rolling their eyes and sucking their teeth as the artists, and mostly the entourage, tried to catch the girls' attention. I seemed to be the only one being chummy with Jay, Damon, and the others. I was in my element. These people were acquaintances of Chuck and were aware that I was G Rap's ex and the mother of his youngest child.

Jay took care of me that day, making sure I got good exposure and anything else I needed. The day went well, although it started off unpleasantly for some. By nine o'clock that morning, Damon Dash had already been drinking. He emerged from the pool house with a bottle of Belvedere vodka in his right hand. He was staggering as he walked alongside the pool, where we were shooting. I watched intently, mainly waiting for him to fall into the pool, but he did not. Instead, he fell about seven feet away from the pool and lay flat on his back with his arms and legs outstretched, vodka still in hand.

"Damon, are you all right?" I went over to him. "Damon?"

He gave no answer. I straddled his body while on all fours, leaning my face close to his. To the left of us was photographer Arnold Turner, snapping away with his camera.

Finally, Damon stuttered, "Yeah, I'm cool."

Jay then motioned for someone to get Damon off the ground and off the set. Shooting of the video was halted while Damon got himself together. That was my first introduction to Damon Dash. Years later, he would play a substantial role in changing my life.

Jay and I forged a silent rapport that day which would continue for years to come. I felt comfortable around him and felt that it was all right for me to accept his invitation to take a ride with him down from the house and onto the beach. We hopped in the back of his chauffeur-driven Mercedes S55 and took the windy road back to the shore of Zuma Beach. He asked me if I was doing all right on my first day and briefly asked me about my relationship with G. We continued to talk for a while until his driver parked on the beach and exited the vehicle. After a few moments of silence, Jay pulled out his penis, covered it with a condom, and placed his hand on the back of my head. I was being a good girl, thanking him and proving my worthiness of the kindness he had shown. I was doing what I had been taught. We carried on in the car for a while and headed back to the set, as if nothing happened, and every once in a while we shared a glance and half of a smile.

Jay and I would remain acquainted over the next few years. As he evolved into one of the most successful and influential players in not only hip hop but in pop culture, we'd bump into each other on video shoots, at events, and at private gatherings. Unlike some of the others, there were no games, no long phone conversations, and no dates. Jay made no professions of love for me nor did he make any promises. It was all very straightforward. It was what it was, nothing more. Since that day in the car, he remained a gentleman and it seemed as if nothing had ever happened between us. And in a way, nothing had.

After my initial introduction into the world of hip hop video making, it was full steam ahead. I began getting calls from the top casting directors in town at least once a week. I rarely had to audition for videos and would be hired strictly by past performances or by requests from the artist. The next video I was up for came one week after shooting "Hey Papi." This shoot would prove to be more challenging than the one before because this one was for Ja Rule's single "Between Me and You."

He and I had not spoken since our relationship went sour. I was pretty sure I would not be allowed to stay on-set once he saw me, but I did all I could to remain. When I got to the mansion overlooking Malibu, I found I was one of the first to arrive. There were very few girls and no sign of the crew or the video's director, Dave Myers. I put my things in the pool house, which was set up as a base camp for the girls and quickly used this time to work on my already glowing tan from the week before. Wardrobe gave me a white bikini to wear. I took my spot in the sun and lay on my stomach on the closest lounge chair. Without a second thought, I undid the top portion of my suit and proceeded to sunbathe without it.

As more girls began to arrive on-set, along with the label representatives and crew, I could hear the dull roar of whispering. The other girls were appalled and the men were shocked, but definitely not upset by my nudity in any way. I knew that there had to be something different about me in order to catch the attention of Dave Myers. It's always a good idea to become the director's favorite and be able to bypass the whole auditioning process and make more money than the other girls in the long run. I had a plan in mind and put its wheels in motion.

I had been on set topless for about an hour when the director arrived. The cameramen and crew were all set up for the first shot of the day. Upon seeing my oiled, naked breasts glistening in the sun, Dave Myers grabbed his camera and began to film. It was film magic as I gave Dave what he wanted. Just the art of it excited me, and knowing that all the other women hated it heightened my excitement and made me want more of this sort of attention. I never really had girlfriends, so the idea of not getting along with the other girls on the set was not a deterrent for me.

There was always someone trying to compete with me and trying to eliminate me—it started with my mother and continued throughout my adult life. On this particular video shoot, there was another woman who thought she could compete with me. I met her in New York, where she worked alongside Irv Gotti, CEO of Murder Inc. I knew from Irv that she and he had been involved. Once Keisha saw that I was on the set of "Between Me and You," she called Irv, and he made his way to the set to tell me I had to leave. He said there was a rumor that I had a plan to have him and Ja set up to be robbed. The accusations floored me and were totally unfounded. I begged him to believe me and let me stay.

Irv grabbed me by the arm and escorted me into his SUV and drove me down the hill to a row of trailers that sat in a sandy patch of land. I began to cry. I didn't want him, or Ja especially, to believe that I would have done such a thing. The truth was that when I was with Ja, I was with Murder Inc. I felt as if I was a part of them. I had a different kind of love for Ja that I will always carry with me, and I didn't want him to think I would turn on him. I told Gotti that I would do anything to be able to stay. I would do anything for him to believe me. I told him how much I loved all of them and considered them friends and would never plot against them.

"If you really mean what you say, then show me," he said, clearly aroused.

Unfortunately, this was a familiar scene to me.

And there in the trailer, I apologized to him for anything I might have done, and even for things I had not—and he forgave me.

After my "apology" to Gotti, we returned to the set together. He let Ja, Keisha, and everyone know that it was cool for me to stay and that the entire situation had been a misunderstanding. I was back in and no matter what it cost me—namely my dignity and self-respect—happy to be there. It was evident to me that Keisha thought of me as being less than her. In her mind, I could easily be discarded as, no doubt, many girls had been before. However, on that day, her seniority over me was overridden. From that day on, Keisha and I would have a silent feud. Not only did she not replace me on the video set, but I replaced her as Gotti's lover. It's funny how back then our disdain for each other seemed important and just, but in retrospect, we weren't that different after all. We were both smart women who deserved so much more than feuding about who stayed on a video shoot and who got priority in Gotti's bed.

The rest of the video went off without a hitch. Ja and I resolved our past issues and even posed for pictures together while I unbraided his hair in the Jacuzzi. I was back with "The Inc." By the end of the shoot, I was sure that I had gained a few enemies in the other girls, but I'd also gained a friend in Dave Myers, who looked out for me professionally.

My next few videos would be strictly for Dave Myers, but soon I found myself working with many other prominent directors and artists in the business. The next high-profile video I would appear in was Mystikal's "Danger," directed by Little X. This single was the much-awaited follow-up to the megahit "Shake Your Ass." By this time I figured out that the only videos to go out for were those that would get regular daytime spins on MTV and BET. Being with G had taught me a lot about the music industry and the economics of it. At this time the budgets for videos were massive, many reaching into the millions. The more popular an artist became, the more radio spins he had, the more MTV and BET spins, the more likely he was to be in the top ten on *Billboard*. Once an artist reached that type of status, even with just one previous single, the budgets became more substantial, and I would do the most outrageous things possible to be in those kinds of videos. Whatever the other girls wouldn't wear, I would wear. Whatever the other girls wouldn't do, I was up for. I knew such behavior would increase my worth as a performer and therefore I would be able to command more money, above and below the table, while pleasing both the artist and the label alike.

On this particular shoot, the conditions were harsh. I can't recall the exact time of year, but it was still chilly in Los Angeles, and even colder fifty miles north of Los Angeles in the desert, which is where we were filming. The location was a western saloon that stood, literally, in the middle of nowhere. The dusty road that led to the location was barren, except for the occasional roadkill, which in that neck of the desert consisted mostly of wild boars and armadillos. It was about forty degrees and the wind was whipping sand around at about fifteen miles an hour. We were all miserable. However, I had a job to do.

When it came time to choose our wardrobe, the stylists had been asking a few girls if they were willing to wear pasties with their Western-inspired outfits and boots. Every girl refused. I was one of the last girls to get dressed. I had been busy speaking with Mystikal, who I met months before at L'Ermitage in Beverly Hills. By this time he and I had been closely acquainted and had spent many days and nights together around town. So, by the time I got to the wardrobe trailer, there were very few items left in it, and nothing that could be deemed shocking, which is what I was looking for.

Then the stylist asked the question "What do you think about these?"

In her hands lay two gold-star pasties. I stalled for a moment to think of the ramifications of wearing gold stars over my nipples. Minutes later, with the scent of eureka in the air, I smiled. "I love them!"

I covered myself with a long, plush, white robe that I had gotten from L'Ermitage so the other girls would not see the outfit I was wearing before filming began. I waited around for hours and even fell asleep while waiting for my scenes. Then, finally, the reveal. I could sense the overwhelming tension in the room as I dropped my bathrobe and hopped on top of a table to dance. The other girls, as usual, were both shocked and appalled, maybe even a little disgusted. But once Mystikal got onto the set and saw my outfit, he gave me his stamp of approval. Not only was I wearing the gold-star pasties, but also chaps, with only an ostrich-skin thong underneath so that my rear was fully exposed. If shocking was what I was going for, I had outdone myself. For the remainder of the shoot, I continued to perform and receive the majority of attention from both Little X and Mystikal, as well as the full attention of the MTV camera crew and a reporter who came to film a documentary called *When Sex Goes Pop*.

Once the camera crew and reporter caught a glimpse of my outrageous costume, all of the attention and cameras were focused on me. At one point, the manager of singer Nivea, who was featured on the single, complained to the camera crew that his artist was the star, and she was not being interviewed, yet I was. It was a testament to the old adage that sex sells.

The rest of the shooting day and the following day went

smoothly. By the end of it all, I knew that I had again created and sustained many enemies within the core group of girls who worked on many of the same videos as me. Most women on video shoots are professional women who are represented by top commercial agencies. As I said before, it is very rare for a principal model to talk to an artist, and many times they look down on the artists. I was breaking all the rules as I cavorted with many of the artists that I worked with, during and after shooting. It meant nothing to me compared to the acceptance of the men behind the production because they were in a position to determine my fate, both professionally and financially. Little X seemed impressed and excited about my performance, and we instantly exchanged numbers on the first day of shooting. He and I would work together at least once after "Danger," but X would play a far more important role in my life. Mystikal was equally pleased and praised me for making his video "hot."

We spent those nights together while filming the video, and he made sure I was taken care of, financially, for "looking out." I was making around fifteen hundred dollars a day for a minimum of two days, but after the "Danger" video aired, along with the accompanying *When Sex Goes Pop* documentary, my rate nearly doubled. I had learned to play the game, and everywhere I turned, I was being rewarded for my devilish behavior. My life had definitely changed since I'd moved to Los Angeles, but little did I know, there would be a big difference between living in Los Angeles and arriving in Hollywood.

Chapter Twelve

A MAN APART

During my first day of work on the set of *A Man Apart*, we shot one of the early scenes of the film. Once again, I found myself at a gorgeous beachfront home in Malibu's Zuma Beach, and I worked from six in the morning until around six in the evening. There was a perfect sunset on the horizon and a brisk chill in the air. Flocks of birds could be seen flying over the ocean as its waves crashed onto the shore. This was Southern California at its best.

I was content with the work I had done and excited to be among the cast, crew, and director. Larenz and I forged a pleasant friendship that would translate on-screen. I would stay in character, as his wife, even during breaks in the shooting. I would make his plate at lunch and nitpick about his clothes and hair . . . making sure everything was in order. There were no actual romantic feelings between Larenz and me, but I enjoyed being his wife for the duration of our time on *A Man Apart*. He was kind and very much a gentleman. On a few occasions, his mother and grandmother would visit him on set. It was easy to see where Larenz had gotten his manners and respect for women. He was extremely grounded and humble, and made my job as a new actress easier.

As a director, F. Gary Gray seemed to be extremely hands-on. He saw to it that all of the cast members became acquainted with one another even before we began to shoot the film. He sent Larenz and me on a few dinner and lunch dates strictly for that purpose. Gary was also very helpful to me and guided me through the entire process. He gave me a few pointers about acting, of course, but also made me aware of my body on-camera. At the beginning of filming, I weighed in at 140 pounds. Gary explained that although I would be attractive to any man walking down the street, the camera would not be so kind and that I should lose weight immediately. And so I did. During a two-week break from the film, during the holiday season of 2000 and early 2001, I lost twenty pounds before returning to the set. How I lost the weight is another story, filled with cold Atlanta nights with a very young lover: Belvedere vodka.

Gary also told me one other very important rule to making a successful picture. Under no circumstances was I to ever date or have sex with any of my male costars. I was the only woman on the set, for the most part, and seemed to stand out with my trademark walk. I had inherited the same sexy swagger that my mother and grandmother had all of their lives. It was like a cobra doing her dance of death, right before the strike of her venomous bite, a form of peacocking I had used to entice men that had become second nature to me. Add that to my 38-C breast size, twenty-three-inch waist, and thirty-eight inch hips and bottom, and it was obvious that there could be trouble on the set.

I took Gary's advice to heart. After all, he did know best. But I have to admit, it was impossible, at best. I had been paying close attention to Vin Diesel while on-set, secretly listening to everything he said and following him around with my eyes. I loved it when he walked past me and hoped he would say something to me, something outside of the work that we had to do. But he remained professional, and I remained desirous.

At the end of the first shooting day, I left the set and walked slowly to the row of trailers that were lined along the beach, beaming on the inside while trying to compose myself on the outside. I couldn't believe I was shooting a film and would actually be in a movie. I was watching the ocean in all its splendor and thought about how far I had come and all the places I would like to go from here. It seemed as if my world had opened up and I'd been given a chance to change my life drastically. I thought that maybe all those days that I practiced my acceptance speech to "The Academy" just might pay off. I reflected on a few of my favorite actors and movies, like Cary Grant in *An Affair to Remember* and Robert De Niro in *The Deer Hunter.* There is something very magical about the city of Los Angeles, which was magnified to its brightest from behind my rose-colored glasses. I began to see what the rest of the world and Hollywood had already known. This is a place of dreams.

I continued my slow, lazy walk down the beach. Busy daydreaming, I passed the production trailer and then Gary's trailer. Without warning, I was grabbed around the waist and scooped into the next trailer. His strong, massive hands grabbed me by the shoulders and pulled me into his handsomely chiseled face. Reminiscent of a scene from *Gone With the Wind*, he pressed his lips firmly against mine, then as they parted, our tongues touched and then danced. I melted in his mouth as the sun began to set over Zuma Beach. Vin and I were breaking all the rules and falling for each other. I knew that what we were doing was forbidden, but it felt so right and so necessary. I had imagined this scene from the first moment I met him but had never thought it possible. He had been changing his clothes and wore only his pants as his bare chest pressed against mine. I wanted to feel my skin and soft, round breasts against his hard, lean muscles. I wanted more than I could have at that moment, but what he was giving me was powerful just the same.

There had to have been some sort of silent sexual tension. The entire time we were filming, I secretly fantasized about us making love on that very same beach. I wanted him, but for the first time that I could remember, I was afraid to show it. There must be something to say about the actions and effects of pheromones because we had no openly flirtatious exchanges. There was no indication, at least outwardly, that it was okay for him to approach me in this way, let alone kiss me. Vin must have just smelled it, like an animal in the wild. The way he kissed me reflected that. The way I kissed him back confirmed it.

After our first kiss, Vin and I spent many days and nights together. It seemed to be a quiet place in his life— sort of the calm before the storm. We were still able to go to clubs, and once we sat outside a club in his black-on-black SUV listening to music because he couldn't get in. No one knew who he was, and I was just getting to know him. We spent a quiet night or two back at my condo, talking in depth about our lives. I remember him asking me about music—about who was hot at the time and which CDs he should buy. I was stunned by how uncool and almost sheltered he seemed to be.

Yet here was this beautiful man with an amazing body, blessed with an enviable eight-pack and an even more enviable sizable penis. His body was perfect, and the way he made love was slow and sensual and thoughtful. Between his gentle, passionate kisses, he frequently whispered "Are you okay? Is everything all right?" always to be sure that I got pleasure out of our lovemaking. The weight of his body on top of mine and the way his hands caressed every reachable inch of me while he stroked my inner core drove me wild. His kisses were soft and just wet enough. His lips were full and warm, and everywhere they went I shook with full-blown desire.

I was so attracted to this plain, straitlaced guy, who had never owned an R. Kelly album or ever heard a Ja Rule record (even after they filmed *The Fast and the Furious* together). I liked him because he was the opposite of me and everyone I knew. He represented a new life that I could easily picture myself living. I found him easy to be with. He was fun and funny. I remember filming one particular scene where Vin's character, Sean, was just awakening from a coma. I sat there, watching him act brilliantly. Just as the camera focused on my face to catch my emotional reaction to his awakening, all I could think of was the first kiss we shared and the good sex we had been having. During every scene that we had together, I would glow in his presence and had to resist my telling grin and blushing cheeks. Like the scene where we were at a police conference: Larenz and I were already there, and Vin walks in with the woman who played his wife in the film. I could feel myself glowing at the sight of him as my eyes stayed planted on his. I felt that it must have been obvious to everyone else, but no one knew. Not until now. I fell for Vin during the shooting of *A Man Apart,* but soon *The Fast and the Furious* and *XXX* would take Vin far away from me.

Just as it is with music videos, there was a separation between the cast and the extras. The cast members were treated like royalty. We would have all meals fully catered and be served the best of food and drink, while the extras were made to eat lunches brought from home and in a separate dining area away from us. That was part of the difference between actors protected by the Screen Actors Guild (SAG) labor laws and those who were not. Extras are usually people trying to become covered by SAG and need to rack up a certain amount of hours worked in order to qualify for its benefits. Although *A Man Apart* would be my first feature, the amount of hours that I would be under contract with the film, and the money I would be paid for my appearance in the film, assured me a place in the Screen Actors Guild. I was officially an actress.

I was doing something that, literally, millions of people try to do every day in Hollywood, and I hadn't even been trying. I have been told by agents and managers to never repeat the story of how I had been discovered because other actors would resent it. It was the sort of fairy tale only heard of in books or seen on television. There are young people, even today, sleeping on Hollywood and Sunset Boulevards who started out with the same dream that I'd had. They walk up and down those telltale boulevards, hoping to be discovered by a passing director or actor. I was discovered on the boulevard of broken dreams and went straight into a costarring role on a big-budget Hollywood picture. I couldn't have asked for a more perfect Hollywood beginning.

But that was just how my life seemed to be working itself out. Everywhere I turned, someone was there to change my life, mostly for the best, but sometimes for the worst. It didn't matter if I was at a Hollywood party or at my local grocer, a famous, wealthy, or powerful man would be behind or in front of me—people like Ice and Gary. It seemed as if no matter the type of mess I'd get myself into, there were certain things that had to happen, despite myself. Everyone I had come across had a purpose in my life, and with the type of breaks I was getting, I thought I was headed for better things.

I was not lucky, but blessed. Being a Hollywood actress, or anything related to entertainment, doesn't happen to many people who come from St. Thomas. On the island, the only focus for children is their education. The only dream is to graduate high school, then college, then join the armed forces and/or get a job. People rarely step outside that box. Many islanders stay on the island all their lives, never leaving, not even for vacation. They are islanders at heart and make those great Virgin Islands what they are— jewels in the Atlantic. Most natives need no more than what those twenty-eight square miles have to offer. But I'd always been a dreamer, though I would soon learn the value of that old adage about being careful about what you wish for, courtesy of a certain NBA legend.

Chapter Thirteen

MISTER BIG

WHEN I BEGAN SHOOTING *A Man Apart,* I was on top of the world, both professionally and financially. Working as an actress in a green-lighted movie meant I no longer had to do things I didn't want to do to pay bills. I was free from having to strip in clubs or form relationships with wealthy men strictly to make financial ends meet. Every week a check for three thousand dollars would arrive in my mailbox, whether I worked that week or not. Personally, it seemed as if I had what many girls dream of as well. Earlier that month, I had begun dating one of the most recognizable men in the world, and although he would not be the only man of such high visibility in my life, he would be by far the most generous.

We had a mutual friend in John Salley (the former NBA player for the Detroit Pistons and then on Fox Sports Net's *Best Damn Sports Show Period*), who had set us up on a blind date. According to John, I was this man's type, and "he is certainly yours." John gave this mystery man the directions to my place in Santa Clarita, just thirty minutes north of Beverly Hills, and I waited nervously for him to arrive. I heard a car's engine outside my window and the sound of a door slamming. My doorbell rang and I answered the door, with butterflies fluttering in my stomach. When I opened my front door, I was floored. It was NBA superstar, world champion, Olympic gold-medalist Shaquille O'Neal.

I had gone out with several high-profile athletes and even a few mega-movie stars. He wasn't the biggest, name-wise, but he was the biggest in size. Shaq's presence was more overwhelming than that of any man I had ever met. Shaq stands over seven feet tall, weighs more than three hundred pounds, and wears a size twenty-six shoe. When he greeted me at the door with a hug, I felt like a little girl as my cheeks pressed against his stomach. My face was lost in his huge hands as he held it to kiss my mouth. Shaq immediately began to look around my condo, checking for what I had and what I needed to have. My place was still very new. The walls were stark white with only a small white leather sofa and black wrought-iron coffee and end tables. There was a twenty-five-inch television that I had gotten from a friend and no dining-room set. I had no pots and pans, only disposable plates and utensils. My bedroom had a secondhand, full-size bed and the sheets that came with it. My son's room was empty. The bathroom shower curtains were purchased at the local dollar store and were made of extremely thin plastic, which failed to protect the floor from spraying water. Although I had been living in my place for a while, it was all but barren. I spent so much time with other people, like Ja Rule and Ray J, I rarely came home, except to pack a new bag of clothes and maybe pay the bills every couple of months.

My apartment was so empty that Shaq reached into his pocket and gave me a couple of hundred dollars in cash. The next day, he arranged for ten thousand dollars to be deposited into my bank account. Shaq was very up-front about the way the relationship would be.

"I won't be able to come see you a lot, so I'll just write you checks to keep you happy," he said. He was charmingly self-effacing about his sexual prowess and wanted to reduce my expectations. He essentially told me not to let his size fool me.

I laughed, thinking it was a joke.

"No, I'm serious," he said. "You may like it, or you may not. Either way, you'll be well taken care of."

I found sex with him satisfying. Although one might have "bigger" expectations, for a man who stands over seven feet tall and who weighs more than three hundred pounds, compared to other men, he was nothing to complain about.

Shaq, or "Big," as he is affectionately called, is reputed to be extremely arrogant and conceited, yet also extremely honest. But I saw him as a man who knew exactly what he wanted and how to get it and made no bones about saying what it was. By giving me money that first night, he was saying, "I own you now." We had our first sexual encounter that same night. It was my way of thanking him since I'd always equated money with sex.

Even though Shaq and I had sex that night, it seemed to be the furthest thing from his mind during the remainder of our relationship. Over the next four months or so, Shaq and I would be intimate maybe two or three times. My most prominent memory about our sex life is of the weight of his body and the enormous amounts of sweat that would soak my body, even through my mattress. On one occasion, I had to turn my mattress over to have a dry place to sleep once he left.

Shaq is known to be a very generous man who loves to take care of the people around him, especially the women in his life, as long as they live by his rules. He changed my life at a time when I was so busy living other people's fantasies that I hadn't paid much attention to my own. He paid for all the things I had been neglecting, and with the money he gave me throughout our short-lived relationship, I was able to purchase my son's first bedroom set and furniture for every room in the house. He did, however, have a few specific requests—like a big-screen television and a larger couch for him to sit on. He said that everything in my place had to be big because he was and that he wanted to be comfortable when he came over. He was very protective. He didn't want me to have to do anything—not cook or clean. At his request, I hired someone to clean my house for me. He said that no woman of his should have to work—all of her attention should be focused on him.

He also demanded that I not go out at all or speak to

anyone, especially not about him. Most women would have been more than happy to accept his rules with no problem and no questions asked. Not me. I was so accustomed to the spotlight and living life my way, I refused to do what he asked of me. Naturally, it strained our relationship. After a few months of trying to work it out, things came to a head. There was no shouting or high drama. We went back and forth in short, clipped messages on our two-way pagers as I sat at the first table read for *A Man Apart*. My mind was barely on the scene we were reading because I was busy keying away in an effort to salvage what was left of this relationship. My attempts were futile because just like that, it was over between Big and me.

I threw myself into my work on *A Man Apart,* and threw myself at the man in *A Man Apart*—Vin Diesel. On my last day of shooting, Larenz and Vin sent flowers to my trailer. I had gotten very accustomed to being with the cast and crew. Now it was all over, and I felt empty inside. I held back the tears as I was leaving the set, and gave out smiles and hugs to the remaining cast members and F. Gary Gray, the film's director. But as soon as I got into my car, I laid my head against the steering wheel and began to cry uncontrollably.

I cried all the way home and lay in bed for the next few days. I hadn't been around my old friends or the music industry for a while and soon began to make the phone calls that would get me back in. I craved the cars, the jets, and the yachts to which I had become so accustomed before shooting *A Man Apart*. I longed for the trips to the islands and abroad, even the shores of South Beach in Miami, and with the money I was making, I felt I would be well received. Maybe now I could be one of them. So I went back to hip hop—to its incredible highs, and very soon, to its devastating lows—but first, there was a detour.

This is about the time I resparked my affair with Irv Gotti, head of the label which housed my former lover Ja Rule, as well as singer Ashanti. Gotti would call me every time he was in town and even when he wasn't. When he called, I went to him. I did whatever he asked of me, and he would take care of me financially for the time that I spent with him and Murder Inc. I was a part of something when I was with them, but I was also a drug addict and an alcoholic.

From sunup to sundown, we were surrounded by XTC and cognac. It was literally there for breakfast, lunch, and dinner. I continued to be depressed after wrapping the movie and began to indulge even more in the dangerous habits that accompanied hanging out with this crowd. There was more sex, more intoxicants, and more unsavory behavior. I was paid to be the bad girl, but as long as I was wanted, I would have done whatever it took to stay in the mix. The things that went on while Gotti and I were together are almost unimaginable to me now, but in the haze of drugs and liquor, it all seemed all right. I was being used over and over again. There was man after man—all friends and acquaintances of Gotti's. I was doing what I was told by one of the most prominent men in my life and now was well rewarded for my misbehavior. It's no secret that Gotti is not the most sensitive person around. In fact, he can be downright brutal. It's also no secret that Gotti was married with three children and kept lovers all around the globe. But I was his favorite. No matter where he was in the world, he would always find his way back to me. His wife knew of me and our relationship. I wasn't in love with Gotti by any means, but he was the gatekeeper to the lifestyle to which I'd become accustomed—and addicted. And because of that, Gotti was in charge.

I quickly became Gotti's showpiece. He would turn other people in the industry on to me. I was his party favor, and I became the new form of "payola" with label and radio heads. Whenever there was someone who Gotti wanted to impress, he would send me to them and I would "take care" of them. One of those people was Sean "P. Diddy" Combs.

It was sometime after Valentine's Day, 2001, just after Diddy and Jennifer Lopez had announced their split. Gotti and I had been spending the day drinking and popping XTC, as usual. The mixture of alcohol and X often made us extremely sexual, and we would have sex all day and night. As a lover, Gotti was insatiable. The drug drove him to unbelievable heights and soon he began experimenting with Viagra. The sex became more like a boxing match than anything else. We would compete against each other, and on most every occasion, I would win. There were a few times when he actually got up and ran and even locked himself in the bathroom in order to get away from me. Still, at other times, he got the sexual upper hand, and I would lie in bed, curled into a ball, feeling completely spent, which in my inebriated state turned me on even more. Gotti and I were a perfect match as lovers.

On one particular night, we were riding around Beverly Hills in a limousine with Ja and other members of The Inc. and we ended up at Mumba, a club on the west side. We ventured through the club, entourage in tow, and made our way to the outdoor patio and out to the back parking lot. I stood there beside Gotti as Diddy walked up to him. They greeted each other with a slap of the right hand; Diddy held a drink in is left. He seemed to be as intoxicated as we were. I stood there looking at him while they spoke, when all of a sudden he turned and looked right at me.

His conversation with Gotti was abruptly cut short as he took a few steps closer to me, grabbed my hand, and said, "I want you. Can I have you?"

Then Diddy turned to Gotti and said, "My bad, Dog. Is this you?"

Gotti quickly said, "Nah, it's cool. This is Yizette. She's cool people."

"Can she come with me?" Diddy asked.

I wanted to leave with Diddy right then. The XTC had me in a mood where whatever I felt normally was heightened a hundred percent. Even the wind on my face made me orgasmic. Right there in front of me, Gotti and Diddy made arrangements for me to meet Diddy at his house in an hour.

"I'll send her to you in a little bit," Gotti said. "Give me the address."

I didn't understand why Gotti didn't let me go with Diddy right then, but we took the address and got back in the limo. We went back to L'Ermitage, and after we took more XTC, Gotti was tearing away at my clothes. Gotti had a strange bedside manner. He would get rough at times, which I could handle when we were high. He also liked to compare himself to other men. He would want to know how they were built and how they had sex. He wanted to know if I liked Diddy and if I was going to sleep with him when I got over there.

"You gonna fuck him good, huh?" Gotti asked.

I just wanted him to hurry and shut up so I could make my way to Canon Drive to meet up with Diddy.

Gotti sent me on my way and gave me a key to his room so I wouldn't wake him when I returned. It was four in the morning when I pulled up to Diddy's home in my SUV. There were security guards in the driveway—all of them dressed in dark suits with their hands clasped in front of them. They stood at attention, waiting for me to approach the gate. They had been expecting me and they let me in the gate and into the house, through the garage. I stood in the hallway, waiting for Diddy. My body was hot as the drugs and alcohol continued to feed off of each other.

After just a few minutes, Diddy greeted me and showed me to the nearest bedroom, where Farnsworth Bentley, Diddy's self-proclaimed manservant had been sleeping. Diddy woke him and gestured for him to leave the room. My guess was that there was someone else upstairs in Diddy's room and that this was to be my first and final destination within the home.

"So who is Gotti to you?" he asked. "And is he cool with this?"

"Gotti's my boy," I said. "When I see something I want, he lets me have it."

With that slight formality out of the way, Diddy and I

spent the next fifteen minutes or so engaging in the usual. After the experience he said, "You're one of the best." I said the same to him when, in actuality, he was average. Our sexual encounter was pretty straightforward, nothing out of the ordinary.

Before I left, he asked me to meet him back at the house the next morning around eleven thirty for brunch. I emphatically accepted and traveled back to L'Ermitage and to Gotti, who was asleep. I crawled into bed and fell asleep beside him. The next morning, Gotti wanted details. I really had nothing to say about my experience with Diddy. He was polite and gentle, and I actually preferred him, as a person, over Gotti, who was cocky and nasty at times. Gotti seemed a bit frustrated with my unwillingness to give details and even more irritated by the fact that I had been invited back for brunch. He always wanted to present me as his resident whore but hated it when anyone actually wanted to keep me around, which happened quite often. He almost relished the idea of people using me and then throwing me away, like yesterday's newspaper. But I was beaming from ear to ear as I got dressed to head back to Diddy's house. Gotti left in a hurry, with the look of disgust on his face. And that made me even happier.

Back at Diddy's, I was received with open arms by him and his entire staff. I met him upstairs in his dressing quarters, where his tailor was fitting him for the upcoming *MTV Music Awards*. I was awestruck by the vast array of suits, ties, shirts, and shoes. They were so obviously rich in fabric and texture, and he was handsome in everything that he tried on. I stood by the French doors, drinking in the sun, as

Farnsworth Bentley sat intently on the floor next to me with his legs crossed Indian style. He looked up at Diddy with a gleam of admiration. Everyone in the home was devoted to Diddy and catered to all of his needs—and, for the afternoon, all of mine.

Brunch was served on a long rectangular table in the dining room. Diddy and I sat and talked about who I was and about my relationship with Gotti. He listened but didn't have much to say. He was extremely kind, and I remember him complimenting me, saying I was very pretty and had beautiful skin. I began to understand all the hype about Diddy, why he is this pop-culture icon. He's got that star quality, that something which draws people to him and makes them want to be in his space and part of his world. I was no different. By the end of the afternoon, I'd become easily enamored.

There was still so much going on during this time in my life. The drug use and drinking got heavier and more frequent. I also began to experiment with different types of XTC. The three major components of the drug are cocaine, heroin, and speed. I began to take the drug in large doses and in different mixtures—some with more cocaine or more speed. It would keep me up all night and part of the next day. Under its influence, sex became more of an experience for me, and I would fall even more "in love" with my mate than I would have done without it.

Every night was a party for me, and I easily became less of a person and even less of a mother. I wouldn't see my son for weeks and even months at a time. My nanny and her family had basically adopted my son. She was the one who potty-trained him and got him on solid foods. She and her family were there for him as I ran around the world, chasing acceptance and money. Pretty soon I was burned out.

It became increasingly difficult to keep up with the lifestyle I had adopted. Ja would call us all "rock stars" because that was the type of life we were leading. They had it all—the money, cars, homes, the girls. And if you were with them, you had it all, too, until you realized that none of them could ever sustain it. It was all just a myth. I could see we were all growing weary, becoming, each day, a shadow of the person we'd been before. In fact, we were not "rock stars." I was an addict of a more dangerous sort. I became addicted to my companions' lives and to all the material things in them. My body became thin and weary. I wasn't able to sleep or eat because of the drugs and the liquor.

Sometime during 2001, I began to reach out for help, even though I was not quite sure what I would do if I got it. On the night before the *Soul Train Music Awards,* Gotti and I had been up to our regular antics—sex, drugs, alcohol, and hip hop. We had popped a new type of XTC. I can't remember the name of it, but it was about four times the size of a regular pill. Gotti took a half, and I, being the addict I was, took a whole one. We then drove to the House of Blues on Sunset Boulevard. I don't remember much of that night because the XTC had taken over before we even entered the club. What I do remember is lying in bed after the night was over. Gotti was asleep and I was lying next to him wide-awake, naked and sweaty from the sex we'd just had. Emotionally unsettled because of the drugs, I called Little X, the director with whom I worked on Mystikal's "Danger" video. It was three in the morning, and I began to talk to him about everything—my childhood, the rape, and my mother. I talked to him about the things I was involved in, including the self-abuse. I was sobbing at times and angry at others. Little X listened intently for the next three hours and offered what advice he could. He asked the questions that no one had ever really asked, and the answers scared me.

"Why do you do this?" he asked. "Do you think these people actually love you? What's happened to you to make you want to live this way?"

I saw then how distorted things in my life were, how unsound my judgment had become, and it made my body shake. But I wasn't ready to face the truth, so I ended the phone call with Little X at around six in the morning, blaming my weakness on the drug.

I have no problems. I'm fine, I told myself before closing my eyes and falling asleep.

By April 2001, just four months after filming *A Man Apart,* I was penniless. My drug and alcohol addiction was costing me around five hundred dollars a day. My monthly bills at the apartment I barely slept in totaled around five thousand dollars a month, and there were three leased cars in my garage, which cost me upward of about twenty-five hundred dollars each month. I had an SUV, a convertible, and a German sedan. I spent extra money every month on lease payments just to be able to switch cars whenever I decided to go home to pack a new bag. On top of the usual bills, there were also trips and shopping sprees, and even though I was being paid by the men I slept with, I found myself spending all of their money and all of mine, too. I had been around the rich and famous for so long, I actually began to believe that I was one of them.

Needless to say, I was completely delusional and irresponsible. None of my bills were being paid during the first few months of 2001 as I traveled around the world in a dark cloud. I spent a couple of months in Atlanta and in New York and was a frequent flier to Miami's South Beach. By the time I finally returned to Los Angeles that April, there was a red letter stuck to my door from the sheriff, and my garage stood empty. All of my cars had been repossessed. My partying and irresponsible ways had finally caught up with me, and I hit what appeared to be rock bottom.

After I unlocked my door and walked into my stuffy condo, my first stop was the downstairs bathroom. Sitting on the toilet to urinate, I felt a burning sensation. I screamed from the pain and leaned in to the wall for support. I had not been having unprotected sex, but I also knew that the effectiveness of condoms and vaginal films, or dental dams, were less than a hundred percent. I would find out days later that the alcohol level in my body was so high that it created the burning sensation. I ignored the pain for the moment as my attention turned to the sheriff's notice. I began to make phone calls to try to salvage what was left of my life. The first person on my list was Shaq. He had been so generous when we were together, and all I needed to keep the condo was two thousand dollars. Stuttering a bit as I explained the situation, via telephone, I then heard Shaq turn me down before I even finished my story.

"But my son and I will be out on the street in a week if I don't pay them their money!" I pleaded.

He asked me what happened to all the money I'd made on the movie, and I had to lie—something about having a sick family member or something. I even cried as I begged for help, but to no avail. I was too ashamed to admit I had spent all my money by living beyond my means and by supporting my drug habit.

The next call I made was to Irv Gotti, and to my surprise, he, too, refused me. I couldn't believe what I was hearing. As I went down the list, every man I called said no. After about three or four phone calls, I gave up and brought myself back to the reality of the situation. I had to pack up and move and do so in a hurry.

Within a week, I had put most everything in storage and had just enough money to rent a car. For the next nine months, I would be homeless, and sadly, sometimes my son would be living out of my car with me when he wasn't at the home of the family who'd in large part taken him in as one of their own. It was as if I were a sixteen-year-old runaway again, except this time I was responsible for a three-year-old son. Bouncing from pillar to post, I became more of a hustler than ever.

From time to time, I would strip at the famous Crazy Girlz Club on Sunset Boulevard. Even worse than that, I resorted to selling my body to men I already knew in the music industry for the money I needed to stay above water. Between keeping a rental car and trying to manage the weekly hotel bill, I needed at least a thousand dollars every week—which didn't include essentials, such as food and gas. On the weeks I couldn't come up with the cash, my son and I would stay with friends or just slept in the car.

There were a few people who were there for me. I found a warm bed and a hot meal at the homes of directors John Singleton and F. Gary Gray. Whenever they could, they gave me money to help me get on my feet, but it never seemed to be enough. For the moment I gave up drugs and monitored my alcohol consumption. I was clean and sober, and, ironically, in need of even more money than before just to keep up with the increasing costs of renting cars and hotel rooms. It seemed as if I were spending money even more rapidly than I'd done when I'd actually *had* money.

On the nights when there was no money, I would park my car behind the W Hotel in the Westwood section of Los Angeles and rest, or on a quiet back road I found in the heart of the San Fernando Valley. There were days when I drove around all day, not having a place to shower or a restroom to use. I would have to pull over to the side of the road or use a disgusting gas-station bathroom. The trunk of the rental car was stacked with the clothes and basic necessities for me and my son. During that winter, we covered ourselves with heavy leather coats in order to keep warm while sleeping in the car. I would wake up to start the car every few hours in order to use the heat, then turn the car off shortly after so as to not waste gas. I would watch my son, sleeping on the reclined passenger seat next to me and cry. I knew that I was the one who'd done this to him, and I was determined to fix it. But the path to salvation was still unclear.

One thing had become clear to me. The people I considered my friends, and even my family, were nothing of the sort. Over the past few years, I had done what was asked of me in order to keep the men in my life happy, in hopes that they would always accept me and want me around. I was the life of the party and the ultimate party favor and show-piece, but now I was a person with issues. When I had a problem and was no longer the carefree addict they had all come to know, they didn't want me around. They began to change. The same men who gave me thousands of dollars for shopping sprees and fantasy sex-capades were now donating maybe two or three hundred dollars to help me in my plight. I was getting less money in my time of need than I was when I was everyone's favorite whore.

To get back in the game and back on my feet, I pre-tended that everything was fine and that all of my problems were temporary. My resources were limited. By the time G left me, I was faced with having to deal with thousands of dollars of debt. And now with the eviction and repossession of my cars, there was no way I could rent an apartment, no matter how much money I had. What made it even more difficult was not having any family or close friends to depend on for emotional support. I had not been allowed to go back to school while I was with G, and without his finan-cial support, I found it hard to catch my footing. I moved to Los Angeles before obtaining my nurse's-aide license. I had office skills and experience working in retail, but no formal education, and working for minimum wage would not sat-isfy my insurmountable bills. To stay afloat, I had to hustle once again. I would soon turn back to the very men who had used me before and wouldn't help me when I needed help the most. I went back to being hip hop's version of a prostitute—sleeping with men in the industry, both artists and label executives, for which I received money.

The man I affectionately call Papa was unaware of what was going on in my life. I sheltered him from the truth out of shame. But he must have known I was headed for trouble. Throughout our time together, he frequently told me that I would have to change my life completely in order to be happy. He was always there for me financially, but I would never ask for more than he offered. We saw each other whenever he was in Los Angeles, and we met in other places, such as New York and Miami.

In October of 2001, Papa and I ended up spending a few days together in Los Angeles. Now back in the game, I was back to my old party-girl ways. I had been holed up at the luxurious St. Regis Hotel in Century City with Eva, a girlfriend of mine and the longtime girlfriend of Ja. She and I had become extremely close as friends and lovers after a ménage-à-trois with Ja in May 2001. We took baths together, popped XTC, and lounged around in bed enjoying the high. When the phone rang on that day, Eva answered then handed it to me; it was Papa. I'd left him a message earlier, letting him know where I was and that I wanted to see him. I left the St. Regis and drove to the hotel where he was staying that night. Once there, we made love, and the emotions of the moment made me weep with satisfaction.

Papa had always been more than my lover. He was easily my best friend and the one person who I knew loved me. Although he had recently married at the time, I couldn't stop being in love with him. I should have been angry and disappointed enough to walk away from him, but he was already in my head and had become very much a part of my life. I spent the next morning with him in the studio as he worked into the early evening. Right before he was to head back to the hotel, I rushed to get there before he arrived. I got a key to his room from the front desk, drew myself a bath, lit candles around it, and sat in it while eating from a bowl of grapes. I was going to surprise him, so I called Papa on his cell to ask where he was. At the very moment he was explaining to me that he was still working, I heard him come through the hotel-room door. Once he realized that I was actually waiting for him in the tub, he became enraged.

He yelled at me about him being married. "What if I had my wife with me?!"

He said I had no right to sneak back into his hotel room and wait for him without notice or permission. He crushed me with every word. I was dying inside and couldn't take the pain. I got dressed and ran out of the hotel in tears. Unfortunately, I headed back to the people who were always there for me, despite what came with the lifestyle. I headed back to Murder Inc.

The night began rather typically, nothing out of the ordinary. I called Eva and agreed to meet her and a few members of Murder Inc. at Mr. Chow. Depressed and confused, I sat at the table brooding over the fight I'd had with Papa. He was my backbone in my most trying times, and now he, too, seemed to be against me.

"I need something," I said to one of Ja's people. "Give me a pill."

He flipped open the inseam of his jacket and pulled a pill from behind one of the buttons. He handed it to me, and without looking, I placed it on my tongue and chased it down with a shot of sake.

I sat at the table with my head in my hands for what seemed to be about three minutes, when all of a sudden things seemed to go very wrong. I began to feel numb and hot all over. The noise from the restaurant began to overpower me and seemed deafening. I turned to Eva and asked her to follow me to the upstairs bathroom. Once in the restroom, I sat on the toilet with my head on my knees. Slowly, I could see the shaking begin from my feet and travel all the way up my body until I could no longer control it. From that point I blacked out, as my body went into a seizure. My next memory is of waking up on the bathroom floor. Eva was nowhere in sight. I was alone, right back where I had started. I slowly stood up and held on to the sink, looking at myself in the mirror. My pupils were dilated and I could feel my wobbling knees giving out underneath me. I splashed cold water on my face, hoping to snap out of the trouble that I was in.

Soon I was on the floor again, waking up from another bout of convulsions. My tongue was swollen and bloody. I made my way back to the sink and splashed more water on my face. I opened the bathroom door and began to scream my son's name into the stairwell that led to the restaurant. My heartbeat was racing, accompanied by a dry mouth and blurred vision. No one was there for me. I felt I would die alone. Finally, a woman came in to use the restroom. She took one look at me and asked if I was all right. I told her I was an epileptic and had been having seizures. Within seconds, the manager of the restaurant was at my side, laying me down on the tile floor and propping my feet up. Only then did Eva return with a couple members of The Inc. After just a few minutes, I began to feel a bit more level-headed. My first thought should have been for my health, but in fact, it was about how this would affect the reputations of the members of Murder Inc. and the unwanted attention it would bring them and the other celebrities in the restaurant, some of whom I knew.

I could hear the ambulance making its way up the street, and before it arrived, Eva and I sneaked out of Mr. Chow and went back to the St. Regis Hotel. I cried all the way there while being held by Remy, a Def Jam employee. I cried for Papa, begging Remy to call him and tell him what had happened to me. He didn't come.

Once I was in the hotel, everyone decided to go to a club, and I was left to deal with the aftermath of my seizures. My head was pounding, my tongue was swollen, and my speech was slurred. I began to call everyone I could. It was about eleven o'clock at night, and I can't remember everyone I called, but I remember calling my dad. His words broke my heart and shut me out farther than I had been already. I told him about the drugs and seizures and that I needed help.

He responded, "It's late. Call me tomorrow or something."

He had never really been there when I was growing up, and although he was there to save me from my mother, he had always told his children that they could never come home again once they left, no matter what. If anyone could have saved me, he could have. I felt as if he bothered with me only when it appeared I was doing well, while I was living the high life with G. But now that I was down-and-out, he was too tired to even acknowledge my desperate voice. I had known I was alone before, but that night it was made painfully clear just how alone I was. I cried all night until, finally, I fell asleep.

Chapter Fourteen

MIAMI ADVICE

AFTER SUFFERING FROM THE DRUG-INDUCED seizures, I spent the next few days in bed at a friend's house. For about three days, I was high and my speech remained slurred and incomprehensible. I began to reach out to the people who I believed could help me. I wanted to talk to someone who would take the time and care enough to help me get better. Everyone I called, however, seemed to be too busy to talk. Everyone had their own lives, and it looked as if I would have to fend for myself. I wasn't allowed to stay where I was for too long and found myself back on the streets again, with my son. By this time, Papa had sent me enough money to buy a car so I would no longer have to rent one.

Once again, I found myself sleeping in my car

and at the homes of various acquaintances throughout Los Angeles. In a strange twist of fate, I found help in basketball icon and businessman Magic Johnson. We were introduced by a woman I met, who was a personal assistant to Larenz Tate, during the filming of *A Man Apart*. She also happened to be the sister of the Def Jam executive who allowed me to sleep at the Def Jam offices after closing time. After I explained my story to her, she felt compelled to tell Magic, who was then her boss, about me and my son. He met with us immediately and saw to it that my son and I slept in a hotel that night.

Over the next few months, Magic, his friends, and staff would be my greatest supporters. Throughout November and December of 2001, he saw to it that my son and I were comfortable, safe, and able to celebrate the holidays. Magic paid for us to stay at the Extended Stay Hotel in Woodland Hills and made sure that there was a Christmas tree with presents under it for my son. Sometimes he arranged for a sitter in order for me to enjoy concerts and parties. Magic allowed me the luxury of relaxation at times, for which I will always be grateful; yet he was not willing to help me change my life. In fact, I came to realize that a life change for the better was no one's responsibility but my own.

I had been through so much over the past eight months of sleeping wherever I could that when Xzibit called me a few days before Christmas to invite me to Miami for New Year's, I was ecstatic. Xzibit and I had met on December 27, 2000, the same day I was first introduced to Dr. Dre at the filming of the "Forgot About Dre" video. During those two years, Xzibit and I shared an off-and-on intimate relationship. I found him funny and smart, and he had always seemed to be extremely grounded, more so than the others. I considered him a friend because he was one of the few people in my life who never treated me any differently, despite what he may have heard about me. Our relationship had been kept private, and only those closest to him knew of our connection. Like many, if not all the men in my life, I loved Xzibit, and enjoyed every moment we spent together.

We arrived in Miami on December 29. When most of the country was freezing, Miami was a balmy eighty degrees. We went to the Turnberry Resort, about a half hour from Miami Beach. Our suite overlooked the golf course and a lake filled with white swans. We were to stay there for the next two weeks at the expense of Loud Records, Xzibit's label. We checked in to our luxurious suite and began what would be the vacation of a lifetime for me for more reasons than just relaxation and fun. We dined at the most elite restaurants, enjoying the finest of foods, wines, and desserts. We took trips to the malls and made late-night runs to the beach for pressed Cuban sandwiches.

We were in paradise, but there was one reason in particular for the trip and that was to attend Diddy's pre–New Year's Eve party at his home and his New Year's Eve bash at the Shore Club. Diddy had no idea that I would be coming, and I hadn't seen him since earlier that year. I had not told Xzibit that Diddy and I knew each other, for fear he would decide not to take me. I was looking forward to seeing Diddy again, and especially to what I knew would be the look on his face when he saw me.

Finally, the moment arrived, and Xzibit and I stepped into Diddy's home. I looked around for a moment and saw a lot of people who I knew, yet I was only concerned with the host. Just as I was scanning the room for him, Diddy appeared in front of us. All of his attention was on Xzibit as he greeted him, thanking him for coming. As he moved down the line, his eyes fixed on my face and his jaw dropped. Diddy said his hellos and gave me a generous hug, then grabbed me by the hand and pulled me out to the front lawn.

Diddy asked uneasily, "We're cool, right? I mean, we're friends, right?" I was confused by the line of questioning, but assured him we were, in fact, cool.

He continued: "I'm saying, though. You know I have kids and a mother and people who love me, and I can't afford for anything to get out. I don't want them to be upset."

I was still very confused but reassured him that I would in no way try to harm him and especially not his family and loved ones.

We went back into the house and met back up with Xzibit. The look on Xzibit's face was asking *What's going on?* and all I could do was shrug my shoulders. I had no idea. I went along to mingle with the rest of the attendees and say hello to the people I knew. Diddy and Xzibit disappeared upstairs, at Diddy's request, leaving me baffled. About forty-five minutes later, Xzibit came downstairs and grabbed me by my forearm, dragging me out to the front lawn. His eyes were wide and his mouth open.

"What did you do to that man?" he asked.

I was even more confused than ever. Xzibit went on to describe the conversation he'd had with Diddy. Diddy had warned Xzibit to be careful around me and to not let me near his home. Diddy even confided that he was in the process of buying the home we were in, but now that I had been there, he would not go through with the purchase. Then he said something even stranger.

Xzibit told me that Diddy said, "She'll have you on video with fingers in your booty." By this point Xzibit was just as confused as me. We stood on the front lawn laughing hysterically. Diddy appeared to be under the influence. But underneath the laughter, there was a serious thought running through my head. Why was Diddy this anxious around me? I remained baffled and threw the thought into the back of my mind as Xzibit and I rejoined the party.

There was fabulous food and drink, and plenty of other stimulation. We were all having such a good time, with maybe the exception of Farnsworth, who appeared to have gotten on Diddy's bad side that evening. We partied until the early morning and were expecting it all to come to an end when Diddy summoned Xzibit and me to join him in heading to a local nightclub. The three of us jumped into his black-on-black SUV, which was a small part of his large convoy of similar vehicles. After a short ride, we arrived at the nightclub.

I do not remember the name of the club, but I do remember what it was like inside. At first, we all sat in the VIP area and cracked open a few bottles of champagne and made a toast to the new year. It felt good to be out with Xzibit and even with Diddy. We were all happy and living in the moment. All of the troubles which awaited me back in Los Angeles were just that: back in Los Angeles. The club was full of energy; the music was loud, and the dance floor was packed. There were several men who were shirtless and the few women who were there were also wearing very little. Xzibit went crazy when we got on the dance floor. Not one for dancing, I stood on the sidelines and watched him. He was so happy, so free, and enjoying his blessed life. I couldn't help but feel a little sad as the alcohol began to wear off. I wanted this moment to last forever—the laughing, the sips of premium champagne, the loud music and carefree feelings.

As I stood and watched Xzibit dance and jump around, greeting the fans who reached out to him, I noticed that the majority of the men around us were gay. There were a few gay couples scattered around the club, kissing and carrying on in dark corners. There were others dancing together on the dance floor, bumping and grinding. I flagged down Xzibit to share my revelation with him.

I asked him, "Look around. Do you notice anything strange about this place?"

He stopped dancing and took a second to look around the room. Soon enough, it hit him, "This shit looks like a gay club!"

I responded with a grin and a nod—this was Miami, after all. My grin soon turned into roaring laughter as Xzibit stood there in disbelief. "Did this motherfucker just bring us to a gay club?" he asked, laughing, and laying aside, for a moment, the usual macho mantle that cloaks most rappers.

Again I responded with a loud roar of laughter. We finished the night at the club and soon made our way back to the Turnberry Resort. It was a night to remember, and we stayed up until about nine in the morning, making love and laughing about the night we had out with Diddy. But it wasn't over yet—the next night would be Diddy's big New Year's Eve bash at the Shore Club.

It was the first time I had ever seen X dressed formally, and he looked handsome. I wore a black, strapless dress with a fish-fin bottom. We were then chauffeured to the event and arrived in style and right on time. I found myself walking tall next to him on the receiving carpet. My back straightened even more as I noticed the young women Diddy had hired to stand on pedestals on either side of the entrance, dressed like angels.

The party started in a large reception area and spilled out to the Olympic-size pool. There were stilt walkers, fireworks, and synchronized swimmers. It was a magical night, and people came from all over the country to celebrate the New Year with Diddy. There was free-flowing champagne and food for everyone. Xzibit and I drank, ate, and danced the night away. As usual, we would separate for a while and mingle on our own, then catch up with each other to report what we saw and who we spoke to. The night was filled with endless laughter and euphoria.

By this time I had not used drugs since my seizures two months earlier, and even though most everyone around me indulged in XTC, I stayed away. I did indulge, and maybe even overindulge, in the readily available champagne and liquor. By the end of the party, Xzibit and I were eager to get back to our suite and dive into each other. That's exactly what we did, and for the next week and half, we were so into each other, I wanted it to continue once we returned to Los Angeles.

What felt like months away in a tropical paradise quickly came to an end, however. On the last day of the vacation, January 3, 2002, I slowly packed my bags while holding back the tears. I had no stability to go back to and longed for a way to start over again. Xzibit and I sat across from each other in the living room of the suite. I watched him roll a blunt with precision and care so as not to damage the delicate tobacco leaves or spill the last of his weed. He began to go over the events of the last two weeks, recounting all the fun we'd had in Miami. Then he talked about the year that had just passed and all he expected out of 2002.

X had great plans and ideas for his life, and we discussed his business goals and the money he would make and save. He had a five-year plan, which laid out how his career would be built and its effects on his family, especially his young son, who he raises as a single dad. He had it all together and the gleam in his eyes showed his enthusiasm and hopes for the future.

As he came to the end of describing his five-year plan, he looked up from his blunt and asked me, "So what's your plan?" Sadly enough, I had no answer because there wasn't a plan. All of my belongings were in storage and in the back of my car. I had nowhere to live and didn't have enough money to start over. As I sat there, terrified, watching him smoke his blunt, I fought back the biggest cry of my life. The flight back was long for me, as I sat up in my first-class seat while X napped the whole way. My mind was racing, trying to figure out what I would do when we touched down in Los Angeles. The party was over, and I was the only one with nothing to do and nowhere to go.

We pulled up to Xzibit's house and I packed all of my things into the backseat of my car, gave him a long, deep hug, and said good-bye. He had a lot to do and was eager to get back to his life. Though I was longing to stay with him, it was back to the Extended Stay Hotel for me. Once I arrived there, I placed a postcard of the Turnberry Resort on the mirror, next to a picture of my son with Santa Claus, which he'd taken a few weeks before. I missed Miami as if it were my home, and I missed my son, wishing I could give him a home. My life was a mess.

Chapter Fifteen

I CHOOSE LIFE

By February 2002, I had gotten used to living in and out of hotel rooms. I was in survival mode but wasn't necessarily living. I had gone back to being an exotic dancer, hating every minute of it, but I had a little boy depending on me. However, out of the mud came a rose, and I slowly but surely started to dig my way out of that life.

While in my hotel room, just a few days after returning from Miami, I began rummaging through my belongings when I came across a shoe box that had been taped shut. In the box, I had stored a lot of my memories: backstage passes, pictures, airline tickets, and the like. I opened the box and began sifting through this archive of my life and instantly began to cry.

Here I was, in this tiny room, with all my belongings stored in my car and my entire life stuffed into a shoe box. Everyone I knew, everywhere I had been—it was all there, and none of it worth anything anymore. None of it had gotten me any further in life. If anything, I'd regressed and become less of a person than I was ever meant to be. I thought about how it all began and those first few months in Los Angeles, how all my life I had been running from one form of abuse to another, and how, now, I was the one abusing myself.

Sitting on the floor, I cried, and it pained me so terribly that I rose to my knees and began to pray. I could barely get the words out for the sobbing, but I knew that He would hear me. I admitted things to myself that I had never confessed to before and asked God to forgive me and help me get my life back. I begged Him to show me the way and assured Him that I was ready now to listen and to follow. I cried and prayed for forty-five minutes, and by the end of the prayer, I was weak and motionless. I needed help, and the only one who could help me was Him. Within three days of my first real plea to God, I met two people who would help change my life.

I met an attorney at the club and began having dinner with him on the weekends. He was maybe seventy years old, and all he wanted was long dinners at his favorite Japanese restaurant. At the end of every meal, he would hand me an envelope filled with twenty-five hundred dollars in cash. Every Saturday, it was the same deal. He told me there was another plan for me and that I was too special to be dancing at the club. This money allowed me to stay out of the club and to pursue other interests, such as developing my auditioning and writing abilities. To me, he was an angel on earth.

Around this time, I also met a man named Mario. Although I wasn't romantically interested in him, he pursued me intently, and in the process, he became someone I trusted. I was too embarrassed to tell him I was living at a hotel, but when I finally broke down and told him, he allowed me to stay at his apartment. He said he would be moving out of his apartment in a week. It would be vacant and still under lease to him for another month. I was relieved to be out of the hotel and saving the five hundred dollars a week that it took to stay there. So now I was making more money and hardly spending any. It was within this period that tax time came around and I received a ten-thousand-dollar tax-refund check from my work on *A Man Apart*.

A month later, it was time to leave Mario's apartment and to find a home of my own. I had the money, but I had two very serious problems: my credit was ruined and I had never held a legitimate job in my life. When I was married to G, everything had been in my name. When he decided to leave, he also left me with all of the household bills. On the credit scale of 500 to 850, I fell below the radar with a credit score of 416. With all the money in the world, no one was going to accept me as a tenant. It seemed that I would never get out of the mess I was in. I continued to pray and to hold on to faith because I had nothing else.

I was on my way to see a friend one day on the promise that he would cosign on a place for me. I was desperate and willing to try anything. On my way to his apartment, I got off of the main road and began to take the backstreets. I did this out of habit and was, in fact, on the same back road I'd parked on when I had to sleep in my car. Right there was a big bright banner which read APARTMENT FOR RENT with a phone number listed. I fumbled for my phone and began to dial. As the phone rang, I began to think back to those cold nights I'd spent on that street looking into the windows of other people's homes with envy. There was no rational reason why this building's manager should give me a different answer than the others I had applied to, but I felt positive nonetheless. The phone continued to ring as I drove past the building, and then, an answer. With a bit of charm, I set an appointment within the hour.

My nerves were bad and I began to shake. I felt like this could be my last chance. Mario's lease was about to expire, and I didn't want to waste any more money on hotels. This had to work. It just had to. An hour later, a friend accompanied me to view the apartment. It was beautiful, spacious and perfect. Two bedrooms, two baths, a fireplace, everything I needed within twelve hundred square feet. I needed to give my son a sense of security and a feeling of having a place to belong. He had never complained or asked questions. I knew that in his little mind, as long as he was with me, he felt safe. As long as I wore a smile, he would be happy, but I also knew that it was about time that I put my baby first, and this is where I would start.

My credit history shocked the manager. There were thirty-four items listed and all thirty-four were negative. He gave me "the look." I began to panic and basically pleaded for my life. I began rambling on about my separation from

G and how it had kept me from renting a place and about being evicted. I told him how I had been sleeping in and out of my car for nine months with my son and that I had ten thousand dollars cash and would give him whatever he needed to make him feel safe about letting me rent from him. I went on and on until the tears began to fall. The look he had given me a few minutes earlier softened.

After a few days of phone tag, prayers, and more prayers, I got the call, and a day later, I moved in. It was February 21, 2002. God was working with me. Now it was time to handle business. I paid the rent for the next six months and continued planning the next phase of my life. I was determined to do better, to reflect on my life, pinpoint my mistakes, and make them worth the pain. I would start by no longer being identified as Yizette Santiago because Yizette wasn't real. Yizette thought she was invincible, but her behavior led to immense self-destruction that not only tore apart her life but the life of the little boy who depended on her. It was time for me to stop being afraid to be myself. I welcomed back Karrine Steffans.

There had been so much growth and discovery in my life since I had convulsed on the bathroom floor of Mr. Chow, since I drove aimlessly around Los Angeles with no place to live. I was grateful and blessed. There are so many things that the average person takes for granted. These were the very things that I had taken for granted, too, in the past. I would never take those things for granted again. There were days in that car when I drove around for hours with my son strapped in the backseat. There were no rest stops on those days, nowhere to wash up or use the bathroom. We didn't have the luxury of television or video games. We didn't have necessities like food or water. The amazing part of it all was that God had always allowed me to see people who were worse off than I was. I would be in the drive-through at some fast-food place, feeling like less of a person because all I had left was one dollar. And with that one dollar, I was about to buy my son a ninety-nine-cent chicken sandwich. As I dug the nickels and dimes out of my pocket, there before me would be a homeless man or a woman. This happened more than a few times and I began to heed the message. I had a car and there were clothes shoved into its trunk. I had ninety-nine cents, and on many days, I had a hotel room I was able to pay for. I appeared to be a queen to others less fortunate, although I was a pauper to myself.

With my near drug-overdose in the past and memories of Miami still fresh enough to sustain me, I tried to put the celebrity lifestyle behind me and focus on my new life. I stopped hanging out, going to clubs, meeting my old friends and lovers. But as I sat in my new place with all my ducks in a row, I was revisited by that same old loneliness and realized I had an addictive personality. I became depressed and cried every day through the spring and summer of 2002. I drank heavily and began taking painkillers to ease the pain of my loneliness. I wrote in my journal to try to maintain some sort of sanity. I wanted someone to help me, but there was no one left. While my son was asleep in his room at night, I would lock myself in my bathroom. That's where I kept my tools of destruction—a bottle of Jack Daniel's, a knife, cigarettes, and a prescription vial of 500 mg hydrocodone pills. I lay on the bathroom floor, crying, drinking with large, rapid swallows. As the liquor burned my esophagus, I began to cut into my flesh, carving onto my skin the words and names and phrases and people that were swirling in my thoughts. The slicing was so painful, I knew I'd have to take another dose of the powerful painkiller. The room began to spin. I sat back for a moment, leaning against my tub, watching the stream of blood spilling onto the floor. It didn't scare me. If anything, I delighted in the sight. The blood represented the pain leaving my body. I loved the feeling. Ironically, it seemed to make me feel alive again, knowing some of the pain was escaping my raging flesh.

I turned twenty-four in August 2002, the same day that the *Soul Train Lady of Soul Awards* were in Los Angeles. Consequently, a lot of artists were in town. While walking around with a friend, we ran into Ja. I told him it was my birthday, and he invited us to meet him at his house for a little get-together to celebrate the occasion. I was game.

Before going to Ja's house, we drove to Orange County, about two hours south of Los Angeles, for a summer series concert where Ja was performing. I felt happy to be there. Ja always had a way of making you feel as if everything was going to be okay. I sat on stage with his crew as he performed, beaming with pride. It was clear how far he'd come from when we'd first met, when he was just beginning his career. Not many people knew who he was then, and if they did, they didn't give him much respect. For a while we couldn't even get into the clubs around town without paying the bouncer hundreds of dollars. And even then, we sometimes couldn't gain entry. But now this was his stage and all his fans reveled in his star-power performance. For the moment it was 2000 all over again, and I was caught up in it.

Later on that night, we all went to a local sports bar and had taken up four or five tables, ordering about three bottles of Cristal champagne. We drank and laughed, talked and reminisced. It felt good to be with Ja again and to see people falling over themselves to say hello. That was the high. It was like I was good enough and worthy enough to be with someone so adored—yet another lie. I was fighting with myself, stuck between my past and my future. And frankly, on this night, my past won hands down.

The party continued back at the house, and soon Ja and I were in his room behind locked doors. We were drunk by this time and had slipped back into our comfortable old ways. It was like putting on my favorite robe and house slippers. I knew this man. We talked about everything—his life, his career. This was around the time when 50 Cent debuted, and there was still unfinished beef between them. I was taken back to one day in 2000 when Ja called from New York and said he was in trouble. Later that night, he flew into Los Angeles and stayed for almost a year while recording his album *Rule 3:36*. We hung out that night, and Ja told me what the trouble had been. He and Murder Inc. had somehow become involved in an altercation with 50 Cent in a New York studio, and now, two years later, 50 Cent was gaining weight in the industry and speaking out against Ja. As we talked about it, I could see the concern on his face. I tried to be supportive, but deep down, I knew Ja's reign would come to an end—as it does with most artists—and 50 would be his successor, for the moment.

Just then, as she had done a couple of years before, Ja's wife called. I sat on the edge of the bed, sipping champagne, listening to them argue. She was in New York and pregnant again, with their third child. It was history repeating itself. The only difference was that this time the gripe wasn't about me, but about Ashanti, Murder Inc.'s first lady. Ja's wife was positive that Ja was sleeping with Ashanti, though he denied it. Even I knew that wasn't true.

The distraction with Ja was just that—a distraction—and put me in a kind of social limbo. I knew that I had to work on changing my ways, and that change could come only with my continued prayer and discipline. I still needed help and would be, for the rest of my life, "under construction." Still, even as I teetered between worlds, I welcomed my mistakes, because from them would come my salvation. I tried to share the lessons I was learning with a friend— Merlin Santana—whom I befriended in April 2000, not long after I first arrived in Los Angeles.

I had first seen Merlin as a child actor when he appeared on *The Cosby Show,* and at this time, he was a cast member of *The Steve Harvey Show,* playing the hunky high school heartthrob Romeo. When we met, we were instantly attracted to each other and over the next two years would maintain a relationship, which would be more off than on.

In October 2002, I received a phone call from Chuck. He heard that Merlin was looking for me, which was strange since I had not been in touch with him for almost a year. I was curious and needed to know why the frantic rush to find me. Hours later, Merlin called. We caught up on the latest events of each other's life and vowed to keep in touch. In the back of my mind, though, I still didn't understand. It just seemed odd to me that after all this time, he would start this chain of events to find me. There was something bigger in motion, but I didn't know what.

More conversations between us followed, and soon he came to visit me at my home. The first visit was late, around two in the morning. I had just left a party given by Wesley Snipes at his house in Venice Beach. Merlin called as he was leaving a club; I could hear in his voice that something was wrong and I wanted to help. I knew him and his habit of roaming the streets at all hours of the night and early morning. I wanted him to visit me and let me know what was going on with him, with the hope of keeping him off the streets, if only for one night.

After I arrived home, he called me from his truck. I told him the code to buzz himself into the security gate. After two minutes, he still hadn't buzzed. After I called to see where he was, we both realized that he was at the wrong building. He seemed disoriented, so I stayed on the phone and reeled him in. When he reached my front door, he looked awful. He was wearing a filthy white T-shirt that was ripped and blue sweatpants that were washed-out and appeared dirty. His face was oily and also seemed as though it hadn't been washed in days. This wasn't the conceited, meticulous Merlin who I had once known.

For the next three hours, we sat on my sofa and talked. The things he said were shocking, and I realized just how lost he was. Merlin took me back to his abusive childhood— things he had never shared with anyone. I cried with him because I knew his pain. He told me he hadn't been feeling worthy since *The Steve Harvey Show* had been canceled. He thought the cancellation of the show was why he wasn't being respected by people and at the local clubs, which no longer allowed him entry. I saw a lot of me in him—the longing to be accepted and justified; the pain of early childhood abuse; the sense of emptiness within. Merlin would ride around all night looking for places to go, places to belong. He also reminded me of the person I was trying not to be. I began to tell him about the transformations I had made and how I felt that God was working on me every day to make me a better person.

I said, "Find your nucleus and get on your knees and pray. Stay out of the streets and recognize the messages that are being sent to you."

He said, "I don't know how to pray."

I continued: "You have to realize that not getting into the club wasn't a personal attack of your manhood, but a message from God to just go home. Roaming the streets will kill you if you can't humble yourself and ask God to show you what to do. All you have to do is ask."

With tears in his eyes, he told me, "If you and I were

together again, I would have a reason to stay home. You could change me if you would just give me another chance."

His words sounded sincere, but I knew better. I told him of all the things I had learned, thus far, but that I still had a very long way to go. Merlin looked me square in the eye and told me he couldn't do those things, that he didn't know how. It hurt to hear him accept defeat before trying. With that, he was ready to leave.

It was five in the morning, and he left to roam the streets again. It wouldn't be the last I saw of Merlin. The following week he came back. But this time his visit frightened me. It seemed as if those first few seconds we were together passed in slow motion. I answered my door to see him cloaked in black. On anyone else, this would've been nothing, but for some reason, the color was symbolic of his life; he was living in a shroud of darkness. Merlin had forgotten his blue-and-white pin-striped Yankees hat during his last visit and came to retrieve it. We lay on my bed that night and talked some more. He assumed I didn't want to be with him because his show was canceled.

"You'll want me when I'm back on and I'll come back for you."

We kissed that night, as we had during his initial visit, and it felt wrong. I told him that nothing sexual would happen, but I would like for him to stay. He was hungry, and I was prepared to feed him and maybe watch a movie. Anything would be better than letting him go back into the streets again. But Merlin refused to stay, and at five forty-five in the morning, he left my place. He was disoriented, not even able to find his way out the bedroom door. I begged him to stay with me for the night, but only sex would keep him with me, something I just couldn't give him. My life was changing and I knew in my heart that what I was telling him was right and true. God had given it to me and I was here to give it to him; Merlin just couldn't receive it. I cried as he left. Five days later, on November 9, 2002, Merlin was shot dead in the early-morning hours while sitting in a car. I would never be the same.

Chapter Sixteen

DOG-EAT-DOG WORLD

MERLIN'S DEATH solidified the end of an era for me. I recalled the nights that he and I had spent cruising the streets of Los Angeles, sometimes until nearly sunrise. The things I'd shared with him as he cried on my sofa were things that I myself had just learned. I knew in my heart that if he had just been able to listen to me, he could very well still be alive today. I also knew that it was time for me to heed my own warnings and to hear my own advice.

Although many things about my life had changed, there were still many changes left to be made, as it became more obvious that old habits died hard, including my relationship with DMX. He and I had known each other in passing for about a year, and in November of 2002, we consummated our friendship and built an intimate bond. We spent most days driving around town, going to parties, and sometimes just lying around the hotel eating cereal. We spent plenty of nights playing pool at bars and flying model airplanes with my son at the park. DMX is notorious for his erratic style of driving. He would easily punch eighty miles an hour around a bend and never wore a seat belt, stating "It's not accidents that kill people. Seat belts kill people." At one point I was so afraid for my life that I opted to jump out of the Mercedes CLK he was driving as it approached a red light, rather than ride with him.

I remember him saying to me during a fight, "You ain't never met a nigga like me, 'cause if you'd ever met a nigga like me, you'd be in love!" He was right. I had loved him from the moment we met. But I was also very aware of how dangerous that love could be if I took it seriously. Aside from his usual antics, D was actually sweet and loving. He was always with me, by my side, kissing and hugging me. I would tell him, "I need some love," and he would stop whatever he was doing to hold me and kiss my face. On one occasion, while we were out at the Saddle Ranch restaurant on Sunset Boulevard, he bought me one hundred roses. He had a way about him that made me feel special. He began to refer to me as "The Baby," and I felt protected and cared for. He accepted me for what I had been and loved me just the same.

We had an explosive sex life and an even more explosive relationship. During sex, he would growl, scratch, and bite like a dog, and then whimper at orgasm. It was so unusual, so animalistic, it turned me on. It wasn't uncommon for those around us to see us fight. During a meeting with video director Joseph Khan, D and I began to argue about another woman he was seeing. I grabbed all the tiny liquor bottles from the minibar and hurled them at D's head. Quite the ducker, he managed to dodge every single one. Our guests were in awe. The fight carried on into the lobby, where I threw Lemonhead candies at his face, as hard as I could. The staff at the Los Angeles W Hotel came to know us for our raving and sometimes comical arguments.

We grew closer over the next three years, even spending Thanksgiving of 2004 together. Still, no matter how close D and I became, he was still a married man who had many other women. No matter how special he made me feel, there were a lot of women in his life who felt the same way I did. Our sexual relationship has long since ended, but from time to time we can still be seen tearing up the streets of Los Angeles—with our combustible yet reliable friendship and chemistry, one based on unconditional acceptance.

While the majority of the late nights were gone and I was living a more stable lifestyle with my son, my inner demons still ate at me. I would drive my son to preschool each morning—just like the other moms. My writing became a welcome relief from my own thoughts. Putting everything on paper cleared some of the inner conflict I was experiencing. Slowly, some normalcy crept into my life. I was home every night for dinner and there to read my son a bedtime story. But when he was asleep and the house was quiet and all the chores of the day were done, I felt an incredible emptiness. I spent most of those nights crying, depressed and lonely. I was paying the toll for all the years of misjudgments in my life.

Though I had given up cutting myself, the loneliness still ate away at me. I filled the emptiness with another body—Bobby Brown. Bobby was a longtime associate of G and Chuck, but it was Irv Gotti who introduced us, in his same way that he "introduced" me to Diddy. We met on October 16, 2002, and from that day, he did everything in his power to spend time with me in Los Angeles. Bobby was loving and generous. Our relationship didn't last long because in addition to his high-profile marriage to Whitney Houston, I also realized that there was a serious problem. I never witnessed him use drugs, but I did witness behavior which made me think if he wasn't on drugs, he needed to be committed. Bobby would nod off at the oddest times. I remember talking to him while he sat on the toilet, nodding off continually during the conversation. I knew something wasn't right, but it would take a while for me to figure out just how wrong things were.

I easily became part of Bobby's Los Angeles circle, including his goddaughter, whom I had known for years before meeting him. He had plenty of friends in Los Angeles, and they would help us keep in touch while Bobby was back in Atlanta, where he and Whitney have a home. His brother, nephews, and bodyguards were all aware of our relationship. Even his oldest son, who lives in Los Angeles, knew about me. Eventually, I was told that Whitney had become very aware of our relationship as well.

Bobby and Whitney were going through what seemed

to be a brief separation. She spent months at the side of her ailing father in New Jersey. While Bobby was left to fend for himself, he and I found ways and reasons for him to come to Los Angeles to spend time with me.

We spent a couple of weeks at the Ritz in Marina Del Ray, a waterfront community just twenty minutes south of Beverly Hills. The staff at the hotel addressed me as "Ms. Brown." I can't imagine what they must have thought. Bobby and I casually and publicly traipsed through the hotel hugging, kissing, and carrying on. We would have dinner with friends as well as with his oldest son and nephews. We had lunch at beachfront restaurants, in plain view of the world, and on one occasion, we fed each other raw oysters for two hours at a popular seafood restaurant close to the Santa Monica pier. He never missed an opportunity to tell me he loved me, and my eyes would dance as I returned the notion. But there were still many things about Bobby that worried me.

While we were at the Ritz, I was going through Bobby's pockets in order to grab some money for the dinner I had just ordered. In his pocket, I found an ATM card with only his wife's name on it. I also found an ATM receipt which showed the checking-account balance to be a little less than fifteen thousand dollars. This was the first clue that things weren't what they seemed with him. He told me he had plenty of money and access to all of his wife's money. But this ATM receipt showed that he was actually on a pretty tight leash, at least while he was away from home. He even said he was going to find a home to be closer to me in Los Angeles.

After I found the ATM card, Bobby walked into the room in a state of confusion. It was February of 2003, and we had just spent Valentine's Day together. He and Whitney were on the phone arguing about a headline that had appeared in the *National Enquirer,* which told the true story of a fight they'd had in the Bahamas sometime before. Bobby believed most of the stories were planted by people sympathetic to her. And he was tired of everyone saying he was the one who got her hooked on cocaine.

"I don't want to do drugs anymore," he said.

All of a sudden all of his habits and strange, erratic behavior began to make sense to me. Again, I have never seen him do drugs, but his words provided clarity for me. Bobby would cry at times for no reason and he often said he needed a way out. He was clearly very unhappy.

Bobby then walked out of the room and stayed gone for almost two hours. When he returned, he seemed to be under the influence of something and began speaking nonsense. He told me he was a member of Al Qaeda and that President Bush was looking for him. He said he knew where Osama Bin Laden was and who was behind the September 11 terrorist attacks. He also said he and I had to board a private jet right away and head to the Middle East.

He went on like this for a couple of hours, until four in the morning, and I was ready for bed. My son had been sleeping in the other bedroom, and I didn't want to start a fight and wake him. So I listened until I couldn't stand it any longer.

"I'm not listening to this bullshit anymore!" I then screamed.

Bobby got irate and told me to get my son and get out. Here he was making up delusional stories at four in the morning, and just because I didn't feel like entertaining his bullshit, I was being disrespected. So I did what any woman in my position might do—I slapped Bobby in his mouth with all my might. He calmed down and eventually fell asleep, but I wondered how much more I could take.

I had become such a staple in the life of Bobby Brown that he had told his mother about his "girlfriend in L.A.," and I was even allowed to call him at the home he shared with Whitney in Atlanta. On one occasion, he and Whitney were in Los Angeles together and staying at the Bel-Air hotel. She had a very bad cold and cough, and was in the room with him when I called.

He answered the phone and I said, "Come see me." He began to say that it would be impossible, but I demanded.

"Okay, baby," he said.

A couple of hours later, he was with me at my house. We stood in my kitchen making dinner together and later watched a movie while lying in bed. He stayed the night and went back to his wife in the morning. I loved Bobby and he loved me at the time, and everyone around us knew and accepted it for what it was. Yet toward the end of our relationship, reality began to set in. At one point, while we were staying in the Ritz, Bobby had run out of money and we were all kicked out of the hotel. It went downhill from there. He began to treat me badly from time to time, and when I cried about it, he would once again become the loving, sensitive man he'd been when we first met. We went back and forth until I finally left Bobby in April of 2003.

We had been staying at L'Ermitage. Every day we fought and made up. I left for one night to get my head together. The next morning I received a phone call from one of Bobby's oldest friends telling me he had been with a known hooker the night before. I'm not sure what happened, but what I heard made my stomach turn. I hurried over to the hotel and waited in the lobby for Bobby to come out of his room. Two hours later, he appeared and I handed him a note. Among other things, the note said, "It's time for us to go our separate ways." What we had together had been wrong from the start, and I needed to move on.

Bobby had actually grown during our six months together. He would often tell me that I made him want to be a better person, and now he was. He was clean and sober, as far as I knew, and was looking better than ever. I like to think I helped him clean up his act a little, but Bobby did something for me as well. Our relationship left me exhausted, and it was the last time I would start a relationship with a married man. As much as I hated to admit it, I was following the same path as my mother, I was repeating the cycle of being used and reused, and allowing it. Bobby was the last straw. He watched me walk toward my car as he hopped in his SUV and drove behind me. I did not look back.

Just a few days later, after Bobby and I finally split, *A Man Apart* premiered at Grauman's Chinese Theatre in Hollywood, two and a half years after filming. I had been fitted and styled for the event, just as I had been for many other events around town. By this time I'd hired a publicist for the months leading up to the premiere in order to generate publicity and acquire invites to all the top Hollywood parties and premieres. I became well versed in the craft of styling and red carpet behavior. Essentially, I was ready for the evening, yet I felt inadequate. I wasn't at all excited about the *A Man Apart* premiere and decided not to go. I didn't feel pretty or much like of a movie star, so I lay in bed drinking a couple of Corona beers. After about an hour, and just twenty minutes before the start of the red carpet arrivals, I found the courage to get dressed, smear on some lip gloss, and drive myself to Grauman's. I parked my Mustang in the underground garage at the Hollywood and Highland complex, and took the long walk to the red carpet. Nothing about that night, thus far, had made me feel like a star—not until the paparazzi began snapping their cameras and calling my name.

I spent the first forty-five minutes after my arrival on the red carpet having my picture taken and talking to press people from the likes of *Entertainment Tonight*, *Access Hollywood,* and *Extra*. I began to feel confident and beautiful, and was happy to see all of my fellow cast members. I was especially happy to look over my shoulder and see my friend Magic Johnson giving me the thumbs-up and saying, "Good job." The premiere gave me a sense of grand accomplishment that fulfilled me more than any man ever could.

The premiere was not the first time that I'd seen *A Man Apart,* but coupled with the excitement and ambience of the night, seeing myself on screen made me proud. Vin and I shared a long, grinding hug before the viewing of the film and made plans to meet after the premiere and the post-premiere party. I was floating on air, and that tiny taste of independence and professional acceptance put my list of goals and priorities into high gear. I started to form a plan and began to feel stronger and more secure on my own.

I was determined to find success and to be happy alone. I knew there had to be other women who have felt empty and confused all of their lives, and I thought if they could make it on their own, so could I. I began to get my finances in order so I could clean up my credit. Determined not to need a man for anything, I opened my own massage company, employed a few women and men, and saved the bulk of my earnings. I could see myself becoming more of the woman I was hoping to be.

Over the next few months, I continued to be focused and to work hard toward my personal and professional goals. Life became relatively boring, which was a twist. I shut down my massage business in order to devote all of my time to writing. I had always kept a journal, but now I started to write about the events that had led me to this moment. Papa, who remained a friend and confidant, chipped in when necessary and made sure things were taken care of if I needed his help. It felt good to have someone who really knew me and supported me all the way. Although we had our disagreements and occasional fall-outs, Papa had never once judged me, and unlike everyone else, he stood by me through the dreamlike highs and the devastating lows of my past

Chapter Seventeen

SUPERHEAD™

AFTER I BEGAN TO WRITE, I shared my ideas with Damon Dash while visiting him one afternoon at the Beverly Hills Hotel. Although Damon and I had been casually acquainted over the past three years, there was a lot about me he had never known. I started to tell him about my life and why I wanted to write about it, and his face froze with shock. I was still unsure about the idea of writing and didn't know if my life story would appeal to other people, but as I began to tell it to those around me, their reactions said it all. Damon immediately called Fox Search-light, and the very next day, a Fox executive met with us and brought director Ben Younger, of *Boiler Room*, to meet me and hear my story. Everyone was fascinated and sure that this could be translated into a motion picture.

Soon I was telling the story to Shakim Compere, manager and business partner to Queen Latifah. He, too, was amazed and convinced that my story would make a good motion picture. Not too long after telling Shakim, I repeated my story to well-known music executive Andre Harrell while sitting poolside at the St. Regis Hotel in Los Angeles. Again I was met with enthusiasm, but it was Andre who insisted that my life story would be better served as a book. I was doubtful and afraid; writing a book seemed such an intimidating idea. But every time I saw Andre after our talk, usually at the Four Seasons' popular Sunday brunch, he would insist, "You need to write that book."

I was telling some of the most influential men in the entertainment business about my life and my idea of writing about it, and they were unanimous in their opinion. It was necessary to write my story because I had something to say, and it should he heard by young women everywhere. I became more confident and convinced I could make this happen, with a little help from my "friends."

The following December, I was called to do a spread for *Smooth* magazine's "Hollywood Swimsuit" issue, in connection to my appearance in *A Man Apart*. I took the opportunity to briefly mention my upcoming project and a bit about my life, hoping it would start a small buzz that would eventually get the ball rolling. Every night I would sit up in bed and go over my plan. There was a way for me to harness the pain and mistakes in my life to warn others to stay away from the lure and seduction that had gripped me. This marked the beginning of a new era in my life, and suddenly the pain of my past didn't haunt me as much. I could finally see my five-year plan, just as Xzibit had seen his during our fateful Miami trip. By the time Christmas came around, I could see a definite change on the horizon.

In February of 2004, the "Hollywood Swimsuit" issue of *Smooth* magazine hit newsstands. Other magazines—*Vibe* and *XXL*—followed. The shoots were fun, but more important, I used the exposure as a way to launch another business. My partner, Smart Girl Productions, and I trademarked and incorporated the term *Superhead*, which I learned has a different connotation abroad—a positive one, affiliated with higher learning, especially in the UK—and formed an apparel line bearing the name.

Taking ownership of my life felt good. Instead of hiding from my past, I wanted to face it and show other women that no matter how one's life may have started out, it's never too late to grow and to change. Ironically, my darkest days would be the fuel for this new fire in my life. Finally, I wasn't dependent on others for a purpose and would soon learn that wealth is internal. Even with the fast-paced flashiness of my past, I was never comfortable in my own skin. That's what mattered most—not the things that adorned my skin, but how I felt in it.

Chapter Eighteen
USHERING IN

During my transformation, many old acquaintances were being left behind as new ones took their place. But one night, what was old became new again in the form of Usher Raymond.

In November 2004, I was dining with an acquaintance at the Los Angeles W Hotel restaurant and lounge, and I decided to leave at around one in the morning. As I walked down the front steps and toward the valet, I stopped and looked up to see if my guest was behind me. He stood at the top of the stairs talking, and just then, someone came out of the W and motioned for me to walk toward him. As I approached this stranger, he introduced himself to me.

"Hi, my name is Keith and I work for Usher.

Usher's in the building right now and would like to speak to you for a moment, if you would follow me."

Usher and I spoke for just a couple of minutes that night as we stood in the middle of the heavily guarded VIP section of the W's bar and restaurant. I noticed that we were being watched, so I gave Usher my number and told him to call me the next night—which he did.

Usher and I had first met back in 2000 on the steps of that very same hotel. I was leaving after having had dinner and he was just checking in.

"Where are you going?" he asked softly as we crossed paths.

I replied, "With you," and made an immediate U-turn.

Usher and I spent the next several months together whenever he was in Los Angeles. What I remember most about our time together is taking breaks for long talks and bouts of laughter, eating Subway sandwiches in bed and ordering late-night room service, logging in long nights at the studio, watching him belt out singles for his then up-coming album *8701*, making love every chance we could get. He was twenty years old then, and I was twenty-one. Usher was quiet and very attentive, always asking if I was all right or if I needed anything. He was a simple man, with-out the constant security and Maybach Mercedes-Benz he travels with now. When he wasn't in Los Angeles, we fre-quently kept in contact via telephone and two-way pager. He became a part of my life, and my feelings for him con-tinued to grow until he fell in love with Chilli, one third of the group TLC. Over the next two years, as he and his rela-tionship with Chilli matured, Usher and I lost touch.

After reuniting in late 2004, Usher and I began to see each other once again. I instantly saw a change in him and in the dynamics of our relationship. The soft and tender person I had known before was still there, but was often superseded by his more aloof side. I would be drawn in by his tender words and touch, only to be pushed away in a moment of cold reaction. On one particular night, I spent an hour or two in the lobby of his hotel having drinks with his manager, personal assistant, and younger brother, James. Usher joined us, and after a while he and I ventured upstairs to his suite. Turned on by his presence, I ripped off his clothes, dropped to my knees, and ravished him. Usher seemed to be turned on by commanding me to do things sexually in a tone I found condescending and disrespectful.

He stopped me from pleasuring him and began to question why I was there. He seemed under the impression that I hadn't found love, that I was lost and confused in life. But he was wrong. The old Karrine might have been looking for love, for salvation, but the new Karrine saw the search for what it was. I wasn't here because I was lonely or looking for my next high—emotional or otherwise; I was here because, given our past history and the friendship I believed we shared, I felt free to be adventurous with him.

I wanted him to be the same man I had known five years earlier, but was surprised to find him much cockier and more withdrawn. He and I often battled for control of the situation. Many times we would have loud, uproarious fights. I remember the time his twenty-year-old brother, James, and I had been playfully flirting all night as a sort of running joke. From what I could tell, Usher took that as a sign that I wanted James and, spitefully, offered me to his brother.

"I saw you guys flirting, so why don't you just give him what you were going to give me."

I shouted, "If I wanted to fuck your brother, he'd be fucked. I don't need your permission!"

As he was screaming "Bitch, get the fuck out!" I was already out of the door and down the hall. As the elevator doors opened, I took my first step into it, only to be dragged back by Usher. I felt he was playing a mental tug-of-war with me, and it seemed to be turning him on. It wasn't the sex he wanted me for, it was the emotional manipulation. As usual, the night ended with apologies as we lay together on the couch, my head on his chest. For the time being, my tender friend was back.

That type of disrespectful behavior would continue, and every time I saw him would be worse than the last. We fought and made up over and over again. As a result, my relationship with Usher became more stressful. Being with him had initially been comfortable and familiar. I genuinely liked him and felt he was a beautiful man, inside and out, despite the changes that had come with his success.

On December 23, 2004, I received a call from Usher's personal assistant and manager telling me they were planning a surprise for him, and I was eager to participate. The three of us piled into a black BMW 760 V12, and I disrobed in the backseat and adorned myself with a hotel robe. We drove to the set of *Dying for Dolly,* the movie Usher was in the middle of filming. I waited in the backseat as the guys went to fetch Usher from his trailer. As Usher piled into the backseat, he smiled as his eyes became focused on my naked body. Yet he didn't seem very surprised. Per my request, Usher's song "Lovers and Friends" played over and over as we pulled off and headed to the Century City Plaza Park Hyatt.

I instantly took all of him into my mouth. He was immediately aroused and lay back in ecstasy while touching my most intimate parts. I'd had more than my share of martinis at the bar before arriving on the set, and it seemed as if I reached my sexual peak all at once, in the backseat with him. With every touch, I shivered. With every lick, he squirmed. I was ready, and so was he, and before we knew it, we had arrived at the hotel.

The driveway of the hotel was full of college students from Michigan State, who were in town for the Rose Bowl, not to mention hotel staff, guests, and visitors. Still, there was no hesitation as Usher and I walked into the hotel side by side. He held his head high as I walked beside him, holding the bathrobe together with just one hand, and my hair a mess. We were being obvious and Usher loved it.

In the hotel room, everything was just as usual. We enjoyed each other's company at first, and then came another one of his talks. He was working so hard to build me up then belittle me, when all I wanted to do was share some time with my lover and friend. Then, to add insult to injury, after our simultaneous orgasms, Usher walked out of the suite, without saying a word to me. I found out he was with another woman in the suite next door. I had had enough. He was no longer the man I had known five years before, and I was worth more than he would ever be willing to give. I gathered my things and went home.

EPILOGUE

ALTHOUGH THE QUALITY OF MY LIFE has changed,
I still enjoy an exciting lifestyle with celebrity col-
leagues, friends, and lovers. The difference is that
now I am my own woman and look for no one to
complete me. I make my own living and am fully
aware of my worth. Still, my life is not perfect, and
naturally, I make mistakes—from which I can only
hope to learn.

My life has been an amazing ride, and there are a
lot of things that had to be done to get to the point
of peace and acceptance where I am now. By the
grace of God, I made it through a traumatizing childhood, went from being an exotic dancer and a
teenage runaway to being a wife and mother in just a
few short years, all before I'd turned twenty years

old. I escaped death at the hand of a tyrant husband only to be thrust into the dizzying grip of the Los Angeles partylife. I was loved by a then self-proclaimed pimp, seduced by an entire industry, and consequently got so caught up that I was convinced I was one of them—a star with seemingly endless reserves of wealth, access, and power. It couldn't have been farther from the truth.

I was also in love with love and all the stories I had heard and read about it. I needed it so badly that I settled for a love of my own creation and imagination too many times. In my heart, I had loved them all, and it is clear to me now that none of them had ever loved me.

I have lived the kind of life which could easily have killed some people and driven many others insane. I am a strong believer in the adage "To whom much is given, much is required." As I grow older, I realize that I *had* to go through it all in order to reach my destiny in life. I had to be who I am in order to help the thousands of young girls who write to me on my website to ask for advice. I used to pity myself, but now I rejoice in who I have become and am excited about who I will be.

Sure, I still have my connections and acquaintances in the business of entertainment, but now I only do things that add happiness to my life. It's easier for me to walk away from things and people that don't uplift me. And, finally, I am in love, and it has nothing to do with the man in my life or any other man I have ever come across. I'm in love with my son and the life that we have together.

Life is normal now, and I no longer crave the lifestyle I used to. There are Blockbuster movie nights and dinner parties at home with friends; PTA meetings and birthday parties for my son and his classmates; watching him play football on Saturdays and lazy Sundays in bed with nowhere to go—and it feels good.

Would I do it all again? Yes. If someone told me that I would *have* to relive my entire life in order to be as fulfilled as I am now, then I would. I am stronger for it and I am able to be who I was always meant to be. I find incredible hope in the people who have been inspired by my life and whose lives have inspired mine.

Karrine's Grandmother Speaks

VIVIAN OVESEN, *Karrine's maternal grandmother who is referenced in the book and who was largely present during Karrine's childhood in St. Thomas, was asked to share her feelings on the publication of* Confessions of a Video Vixen *and Karrine.*

How do you feel about Karrine and her success with *Confessions of a Video Vixen?*
Karrine's family and friends here in St. Thomas are extremely proud of her and all she has accomplished. So many people go through their lives with the weight of their secrets and lies, never being completely happy—especially women, who often end up bitter as we grow older, unable to receive or give love. For the rest of her years on this earth, she will be lighter in her journey and when she is a very old woman, and goes home to God, she will not go with the weight of her sins on her back.

Karrine writes in her book that she's always loved to perform and write. Are you surprised that she is now a bestselling author?
From the time she was small, this is all Karrine ever wanted to do. She would write and perform her own plays and poetry around the island at big events, for the gover-

nor and local schools . . . winning awards for most everything she had done. I was there with her when she was dreaming of becoming a writer of books, and to see her accomplish this so early in her life makes those of us who supported her very proud. God knows so many of us women have pasts that may be repulsive to others, but how many of us who have been misguided, abused, and abusive can admit it, write about it, and publish it for the whole world to read? How many of us are honest with ourselves about ourselves? This makes me proud; to see Karrine in all her honesty and glory.

What do you hope for Karrine as she goes forward in her life?
Confessions of a Video Vixen has given Karrine a way to reach so many people with the message of unashamed truth; the message of letting go of what has been done and starting anew. Never again will it take a man to define who she will be and never again will she be stifled. The world has opened its arms to her and she will give them more to think about, I am sure. She is on her own now and no one needs to take care of her. The way it all works out in the end proves that confession *is* good for the soul.

Author Q & A

Your address book must read like a Who's Who of the entertainment world. You know a lot of celebrities from the hip hop, sports, and movie industries, some of whom grace the pages of *Confessions of a Video Vixen*. Why write a book about your encounters with them now?
Confessions of a Video Vixen is not a book about my encounters with celebrities, or anyone else for that matter. It is my life story, thus far, which just so happens to include some people you may have heard of. *Confessions* is a story of a maladjusted young girl

who grew into a confused and misguided young woman. It's a story of failure and triumph with the message that how one's life begins doesn't determine where one's life will go.

The cover copy calls this a "cautionary tale." Whom do you want to caution? And what do you want to caution them about? *Confessions* is a story for the masses. There is something in it for everyone; however, I hope to influence those who may be a bit like me: young, impressionable women who lack guidance and self-confidence. I am honored and privileged to be able to share my story and the lessons that are packed into it, such as learning to be comfortable in your own skin and not needing a man or money to define you. It is a story of hardships and the discovery of self with lessons about being unafraid of who you are, regardless of the shame others try to impose on you. Not everyone's pitfalls are the same, but many times the end results are. We all have a story to tell and we should try to help as many others as we can; it's part of the healing.

You ran away from home as a young girl and eventually found yourself seeking fame and fortune in Los Angeles. In some ways this is a classic story. Did you encounter many other young, impressionable women like yourself in Los Angeles? Everyone in Hollywood is seeking fame and fortune; it's in the water here. Everyone from young women to old men—they all want it. I have met a few, and the sad part is that they are still right where I met them. Seeking this lifestyle is like playing Russian roulette. If this is not your fate, it will be your curse.

You've survived rape, physical and substance abuse, and low self-esteem—yet you're still standing. What advice would you give to readers for whom life has been difficult and full of obstacles?

The most important things I have learned through all of this are to never be ashamed of who you are and to not allow what you have done, or what has been done to you, define who you will be in the future. I have learned that it's okay to change and to want more out of life, even and especially when others say you are not worthy of it. I tell my friends, and anyone seeking advice, to decide what you want to be in life, say it out loud, declare it, and spend every waking hour working toward it. We are worth it, and just because others may not see it doesn't mean it's not so.

What do you think of the industry's treatment of women? Is hip hop sexist?

The entertainment industry is vast and is a reflection of the society we live in. I believe what's happening in hip hop now would be a disappointment to its founders, as it's so filled with ignorance and hate. It has done exactly what those who oppose this culture have always wanted it to do—enforce self-hatred among its people. Somewhere in corporate America, someone is laughing at us—at how we degrade our own women and poorly influence our youth. We, African Americans, no longer have slave masters but have become slaves to ourselves through the hip hop industry's recycling of the same ignorance and hate that brought us to this continent in the first place. Maybe that's a bit too political a thought, but it's how I feel. There are certainly exceptions to this theory of mine. There are artists who are truly artists, and those of us who seek more out of our music applaud them.

You have a very nonchalant attitude toward sex; it's almost European. What accounts for that?

I am from St. Thomas, one third of the islands that make up the Virgin Islands. The VI was once a property of Denmark, which is where my great-grandfather was from. The island as a whole, as well as most of the islands in the Atlantic, still lives by European standards. Our education and way of thought and consciousness are very different than here in the U.S. We ran around the beach naked as children, and it was commonplace to see the women of the island wrapped in sarongs and walking around the island barefoot. We are a free people, natural in all our ways. Sex is an inevitable fact of life. It is nothing to be shamed of, or coy about. It is that same shame that prohibits many of our young people from confiding in their elders about sex, and in this day and age of disease, shame can be deadly. I am happy I don't have that shame, and hope to share my openness on the subject with my son, so he will always come to me first.

You credit God with saving your life. Speak to the role of prayer in your emotional evolution.

I've been blessed with the ability to seek a power higher than myself. I used to wish that this would have happened to me sooner, but now I realize the fact that it has happened to me at all is a blessing in itself. I have so much further to go in my discovery of self and in God, and I pray every day for the strength, faith, and courage I will need to get there. Life is a lot easier when you realize that you're not in control of it all. I have learned to be still and to let the world move around me. I have come to an amazing place of peace and acceptance because of my faith in God and prayer. Who and what else can be credited with bringing me out of my own personal hell and to the heavenly space that I occupy now? I have no desire to please anyone but myself and the Lord. He knows I am a work in progress and if He accepts me, who else matters? It is nothing short of amazing when you come to a place of willingness. I have so much more to learn, and look forward to the spiritual journey ahead.